Neworld Review Essays and Book Reviws on Black American History

Book One, Arts and Letters

Edited by Fred Beauford

A Neworld Review Book, an imprint orton Books, Inc

ISBN: 978-1-929188-27-7
1-929188-27-7

Art for Equality: The NAACP's Cultural Campaign for Civil Rights, by Jenny Woodley

Reviewed by Fred Beauford

Changing hearts and mind through art

When I accepted the job as only the sixth editor of the *Crisis* magazine, the official publication of the NAACP, the magazine founded in 1910 by W.E.B. Du Bois, the only real directive I received from the CEO of the organization, Benjamin Hooks, and the man who recruited me, was "see [illegible]can get more of the arts in there."

At [illegible]e, at the very end of 1984, coverage of the arts had [illegible]n absence from the magazine, as much as every[illegible]se. But that was not always the case. Once in its [illegible]y, the *Crisis* was highly praised, and quickly became [illegible] of the most influential and respected publications in America because of political fearlessness, its understanding of the written laws of this country and the unwavering willingness to fight for the equal rights of blacks; and, interestingly enough, for its coverage of the arts.

In fact, the arts quickly became a central focus of the NAACP, founded in 1909 by white liberals, one year before the Crisis magazine.

The author of *Art for Equality*, a lecturer in modern history at Nottingham Trent University in Nottingham, England, framed her book perfectly in the first paragraph of the introduction, which went to the very heart of Dr. Hooks mandate to me.

In 1926, Dr. Du Bois one of the first blacks to get a degree from Harvard University, rhetorically asked an audience in Chicago, "How is it that an organization of this kind can turn aside to talk about art?"

A few years later, James Weldon Johnson, the NAACP's first black Executive Secretary, fully articulated in an article the answer to Du Bois' question. He believed that the "race problem" was "more a question of national mental attitudes toward the Negro than a question of his actual condition."

Later Johnson wrote, "No people that has produced great literature and art has ever been looked upon by the world as distinctly inferior."

Although over the years the leaders of the NAACP fought long, bruising battles over which direction to take to gain equality for blacks and bring true democracy to America, most wholeheartedly agreed with Dr. Du Bois and James Weldon Johnson that what the Negro needed most, beside bread and water, and protection from lynching, was a makeover that would then compel whites to reconsider their negative attitudes towards black people.

The NAACP's first major battle, the book rightly points out, was trying to get the groundbreaking movie, *Birth of a Nation*, banned from movie theaters.

Director D.W. Griffith film, based on Thomas Dixon's novel, *The Clansman*, made cinematic history. Even members of the NAACP called it "a masterpiece," although Walter White, who succeeded Johnson as the leader of the organization, noted "by its very excellence…make it to my mind a most vicious and dangerous thing."

Over the years when I was teaching the film segment in my History of the Mass Media course, I would often show the film (When I was teaching at UC Berkeley a white radical organization called the Socialist Workers Party threatened to interrupt my class if I showed it again. I gave them the finger).

The film was indeed vile.

Woodley points out that "the racist imagery that filled the screen was not just the creation of Dixon and Griffith. They drew on at least a hundred years of American culture for their inspiration. African Americans are portrayed in a derogatory manner, using almost every stereotype in American culture. There are happy, loyal slaves (complete with "Mammy" and "Uncle Tom); foolish comics; watermelon eating, banjo-playing "darkies" oversexed, lustful and power hungry mulattos (male and female); dandified, ridiculous upstarts; and vicious and savage black brutes."

And, as I often pointed out to my often incredibly bright students, the major scorn in *Birth of a Nation* was not against blacks, but those "oversexed, lustful, power hungry Mulattos."

Writes Woodley, "It is no coincidence that the two most important named black characters in *Birth* are mulattos…the storyline betrays one of the great obsessions of both Griffith and Dixon, as well as many white southerners: interracial sex."

I would add to that that they hated mixed race Americans so much because they also knew that these people were their children; their cousins, brothers, sisters, aunts, uncles, grandkids. The One Drop Rule they invented, while it gave some cover, couldn't change that. What they feared most about mixed race Americans, and still do, as you bare witness to all the grief President Obama is getting—is that they saw themselves; that they were looking deeply into their own souls and didn't like what they saw.

These were the kind of blacks that you couldn't trust.

In the end, the campaign against the movie ultimately failed. But it put the fledgling film industry on notice that they would be watched. It also was the first major national campaign for the new organization. It can be said, as it has been noted by a number of historians, that some good did come from the campaign against *Birth of a Nation.* All the national, and indeed, international publicity generated, help put the NAACP on the map.

***

The next major boost for this cultural campaign was helped along by the rise of the New Negro Movement and the Harlem Renaissance. It also produced major challenges to the idea that the arts should be only used for only political reasons.

Woodley points out "the Harlem Renaissance lasted from around 1919 until the middle of the 1930s. This was a period when many intellectuals and artists debated what was meant by "Negro art." In the 1920s Harlem, New York, became the center, psychologically and physically, for an outpouring of African American culture. This concentration of poets, novelists, artists, dancers and musicians was, in part, a product of the massive migration of African Americans out of the South to the cities of the North and Midwest. In the 1920s nearly a million blacks moved from the rural South to the cities. Men and women were drawn to Harlem because of the promise of jobs and the bright lights of city life. James Weldon Johnson called Harlem, "'the Negro capital of the world.'"

NAACP leaders like Du Bois, Johnson, Walter White and Jessie Fauset played an important role in shaping the movement. But the question soon became *what kind of art should artists be producing?* All of the folks I just mentioned were well educated, mixed race blacks; and only one, the composer, novelist, literary editor, song writer, James Weldon Johnson, was an artist in its truest sense; but even he was "grounded in the notion that the creation of 'high' art…was seen as a signifier of a group's status."

Soon, younger members of the Harlem Renaissance like Langston Hughes and Wallace Thurman started pushing back at the NAACP, and especially at Dr. Du Bois, who they came to see as "controlling." They considered themselves artists first, not makers of racial propaganda just to please white folks, and black college professors.

Langston Hughes put it best in his famous essay in the *Nation, The Negro Artist and The Racial Mountain:* "We younger Negro artists who create now intend to express our individual dark-skinned selves without fear or shame. If white people are pleased we are glad. If they are not, their displeasure doesn't matter either. We build our temples for tomorrow, strong as we know how, and we stand on top of the mountain, free within ourselves."

There is so much more to write about in this insightful book, but I will end this review with an observation. In the end, the leaders of the NAACP were proven right in thinking that art could elevate the image of American blacks. But both Du Bois and James Weldon Johnson were wrong that this welcome change in perception would come about through what they called "high art."

They both, especially Du Bois, had a distain for the art coming from the brothels and greasy spoons that dotted black America. Yet, Bessie Smith singing, "Give me a pig foot and a beer" helped bring forth music, lowbrow that it was, that conquered the entire world, and made black Americans among the most famous people on the planet.

Exhibiting Blackness: African Americans and the American Art Museum by Bridget R. Cooks

Reviewed by Fred Beauford

Bridget R. Cooks

The burning question that has intrigued me for most of my adult life is why black musicians, facing the same daunting challenges that native black visual artists, novelists, actors, poets, directors, screenwriters and playwrights, faced -- gave the Europeans a swift kick in the butt, and boldly, and loudly, proclaimed themselves King of this, Queen of that, with additional Dukes, Earls, Counts and

Princes; and the grand prizes of all, the Queen of Soul, the Queen of the Blues, and the King of Pop.

Talk about giving the finger to folks.

Often unschooled, black musicians, undeterred by racism, and more importantly, unfiltered and unmediated, created the sound track not only for America, but an art form for the entire planet that said "America" more than anything else we have been able to create on these shores.

Not so for the poor, unfortunate creative native blacks who wanted to have the same impact on American culture, but who pursued a career in the Visual Arts. *Exhibiting Blackness* brings this fact into full focus.

***

I have already given away most of my narrative by the words "unfiltered and unmediated."

***

Writes Professor Cooks, “In 1927, the Chicago Art Institute presented *The Negro in Art Week: Exhibition of Primitive African Sculpture, Modern Paintings, Sculpture, Drawings, Applied Art, and Books*. This was not the first exhibition opportunity for African American artists; however, it marked the first time that an exhibition of art made by African Americans was presented at an art museum…”

The exhibition was conceived by the philosopher and cultural leader Professor Alain Locke, of Howard University. Locke is regarded as the "Father of the Harlem Renaissance." He, along with W.E.B. Du Bois, was among the first to articulate a clear vision of the use of art, which included literature, dance and the visual arts, as perhaps the major instrument to change the mind of whites that the Negro was “inherently” inferior. He called creative art made by blacks everywhere, “Our first line of defense.”

Later, Locke convinced real estate mogul William E. Harmon to establish the Harmon Foundation, which became the most influential organization of the last century that promoted and exhibited art by blacks.

Locke, however, had a vision of what kind of art his "New Negro" was supposed to create, which has had far-reaching consequences. Notes author Cooks, "The desired use value for Negro art exhibitions to have a transformational sociological effect on race relations is a burden that Gary Reynolds, and more recently Mary Ann Calo, have argued was a prominent tension in the interwar period, particularly symptomatic of Harmon Foundation exhibitions."

The book goes on to list and comment on a number of exhibitions nation-wide, including the highly controversial *Harlem on my Mind: Cultural Capital of Black America, 1900-1968*, sponsored by the Metropolitan Museum of Art in New York City, in 1969. In Professor Cooks' lengthy discussion of the many issues surrounding this event, she manages to touch on all the many issues facing black visual artists: Are they artist first, or black first? Should their work speak to what being black in a racist society means, or should it speak to more personal demons? And, most importantly, do these one-time exhibitions just give the white world a chance to say, look what we did for you in 1969, with no intention of having black artists shown again in the art institutions they control?

And did they, as the present day publishing industry did to black fiction writers, with their separate, but unequal sections in book stores, as well as separate imprints--marginalize the black visual artist to an unimportant sideshow?

***

I think that history will support my notion that Professor Locke and all the do-gooders, despite good intentions, hopelessly hobbled the creative juices of black writers and visual artists, which continues to this day. Art is not Social Science, and is often not logical.

In the end, no matter what the artistic discipline, to call itself art, it must first connect to a deeply felt core of the artist. It really is that simple; and that core is not always about the other, or the "we". Rather, most commonly, it's about one's self.

That's why we call some folks "artists".

***

On the other hand, black musicians were not culturally deprived of all the lively, low-life honkey tonks, the infamous "Buckets of Bloods," the many greasy spoons and juke joints, where no philosopher or cultural leader, black or white, would dare go if they valued their well being.

This was their base!

Also, their art was low rent, with little need of well-off patrons of the arts, pointless art critics and society stiffs like Thomas Hoving of the Met, telling them what to do.

Louis Armstrong purchased his first instrument, a cornet, from a pawn shop. In the words of an old bluesman, about his guitar, “If it ain’t been in a pawn shop, it can’t play the blues.”

The amazing music they created, which kept getting better, year after year, reflected this often grim, often profoundly joyful reality; again, using the same words I used before, “unfiltered and unmediated.”

And that’s how they became the kings and queens of the world.

Amiri Baraka—The Last Beat Standing, a profile by Herb Boyd

There is a sign outside Amiri and Amina Baraka's home in Newark. "9/11 was an inside job," the sign proclaims, and the reaction it has stirred from various city agencies is in stark and disturbing contrast to the pleasant calm that pervades this charming middle-class neighborhood.

The sign may not be in keeping with the general tenor of the street, but to a great degree, it is consistent with Baraka's turbulent odyssey, one that since his days as an enfant terrible in Greenwich Village hanging with the Beats, to his evolution as a grey eminence in a well-groomed enclave in Newark, is as he once wrote "the changing same."

To listen to Baraka, who is just as outspoken today as he was back in the sixties, the sign, like his artistic career, has provoked Mayor Corey Booker to unleash the local law enforcement agency that has been relentlessly harassing Baraka and members of his family.

"Is the sign against the law?" Baraka asked in a recent article that appeared on The Black World Today web site. "And what does it have to do with Newark cops unless they know something we don't! The stops of Amiri, Jr., a teacher at Weequahic High School, Ras, and my wife happened within two days of one another. Arrest warrants for our oldest and youngest sons happened within this same period. When the youngest was arrested and charged with 'wandering,' meaning he had no drugs but was in a drug suspected area. Hey, this whole neighborhood is a drug suspected area," he charged.

Baraka's encounters with the police are brutal milestones marking his furious passage. There is a photo of Baraka with blood streaming down his face after the police had arrested and then savagely assaulted him during the Newark rebellion in 1967. Here's how he described that incident in his autobiography (The Autobiography of LeRoi Jones): "A mob of police surrounded the van, two of them pulling open the front and back doors. They had their shotguns and handguns trained on us as they dragged us out of the doors…'These are the bastards who've been shooting at us! Where are the guns?' one of the cops shouted."

During the fracas, Baraka recognized one of the officers. They were once students at the same high school. But the cop paid no attention to the recognition and slammed the butt of his .38 squarely against Baraka's forehead, knocking him into a state of semi-consciousness. "Now blows rained down on my head," he wrote. "One dude was beating me with his long nightstick. I was held and staggering. The blood felt hot on my face. I couldn't see, I could only feel the wet hot blood covering my entire head and face and hands and clothes. They were beating me to death. I could feel the blows and the crazy pain but I was already removed from conscious life. I was being murdered and I knew it. I screamed, 'Allahu Akbar! Al humdillah!' spitting the rage and pain back at them."

And that incident, that rage and pain is fitting grist for an artist who has thrown himself uncompromisingly—some would say recklessly, too—into the fray of American politics and culture with a matchless passion, and with an incomparable record of accomplishment. Few writers in the canon of American literature have demonstrated such a list of achievements in so many genres. Baraka has excelled in the field of poetry, playwriting, novels, essays, film, music, autobiography, short stories, and performance art. That versatility in the artistic realm is often reflected in his swirling, ever-shifting world of politics and ideology. Like W.E.B. Du Bois, Baraka has pursued his cultural muse with the same intensity as he has given to the search for the right philosophy and the right lifestyle to accommodate his insatiable drive for artistic freedom and political justice.

When I was a teenager, running from something with the same heedless abandon as I was pursuing something else, I used to see Baraka (then LeRoi Jones) in the Village with his wife and children. As if to declare his maverick nature—though at some point love must have entered the equation—

Baraka had a white wife. That was no big thing in the Village because black men and white women, more so than black women and white men, was a fairly common sight. I would see Baraka and the cadre of beatniks who showered him with praise and adulation at jazz joints, poetry readings, in the middle of Washington Square Park, or strolling the midnight corridors, though I don't recall ever speaking to him.

There was something special about him, something that even his cohorts—A.B. Spellman, Archie Shepp, Bob Kaufman, Bob Thompson, and Ted Joans—did not radiate. Joans, with a similar sounding name, came the closest, and it was through Joans that I gained a closer scrutiny of the "happenings," most of which have been lost in a fog of memory, the hallucinogen of time and circumstance.

Baraka's charisma illuminated the poetry readings, the jazz joints and the dens of inequity where such Beat luminaries as Gregory Corso, Peter Orlovsky, Jack Kerouac, Allen Ginsberg, and Diane di Prima delivered their words accompanied by bongos and snapping fingers. Free love, drugs, and bebop only compounded the uninhibited nights and Baraka had an almost god-like standing in a community where craziness was the norm.

Di Prima, one of the few notable female poets in the mix, recalled her fling with Baraka, with whom she once published a literary publication. “I thought of myself as Jones’ mistress in the European bohemian tradition,” di Prima said in an interview. “I had lovers before him, but I didn't fall in love until I met him, and after him I didn't fall in love for a long, long time. He had political commitment and passion. The relationship was creative and inspiring for both of us.”

In his autobiography, Baraka mentions di Prima’s name on several occasions when he refers to her as a contributor to one of the small magazines he published, but he changes her name when recalling personal details with her, including their longstanding affair that produced one child.

Though Baraka was in the spotlight, he managed to retain what most of us had forgotten, and those memories are ably abetted by a veritable paper trail, and a literary diary that has amassed these memories, whether he intended it or not. From the very first stroke of his pen, he seemed, again like Du Bois, to understand that his journey was worthy of documenting, that he was on a mission to leave something of value to posterity. "I have been a lot of places in my time, and done a lot of things," he penned in the foreword to Home, a collection of social essays published in 1965. "And there is the sense of the Prodigal about my life that begs to be resolved. But one truth anyone reading these pieces ought to get is the sense of movement—the struggle, in myself, to understand where and who I am, and to move with that understanding."

The first entry in *Home* is a long essay "Cuba Libre" and it's basically a diary/essay chronicling his trip to Cuba in 1960 in the company of such African American luminaries as Robert Williams, Harold Cruse, John Henrik Clarke and Julian Mayfield. The essay takes up a third of the book's 250 pages, and is a revealing portrait of the island shortly after the revolution; he also offers some insight on the Fair Play for Cuba Committee, the organization that had sponsored the trip. (Lee Harvey Oswald was also a key member.) This was Baraka's second trip to Cuba. He had come to the island in 1955 on a three-day leave from his airbase in Puerto Rico where he was serving in what he called the "Air Farce."

One of the paradoxes of the trip was expressed toward the end of the essay where he said that the idea of revolution had been very strange to him. “The rebels among us,” he confessed, “have become merely people like myself who grow beards and will not participate in politics.” He would soon rectify that lack of commitment to the struggle while relishing the fact that the essay, which was published in Evergreen Review, copped an award and put $300 in his pockets. “That was the most money I’d ever gotten for something I’d written,” he exclaimed in his autobiography.

Then came what he described as a series of “association complexes,” or digging deeply into himself via his novel The System of Dante’s Hell and earlier, and perhaps more metamorphically in his first collection of poetry, Preface to a Twenty Volume Suicide Note. What he heard was the sound of an old skin being shed; he was slowly easing out of the cocoon of a former self, only to be engulfed by yet another chrysalis. It was a painful process dislodging a host of former selves, friends and loved ones in this longing to find himself and the muse of his choice. “African blues does not know me,” he wrote during this period, but he was already moving ineluctably toward a new hymn and a new him.

While Baraka may have begun his research on the material that would become Blues People, as early as the mid-fifties, a comprehensive study of his people’s music, it wasn’t widely circulated and discussed until 1963, and those reviews and comments would soon be swept well beyond “the embrace of the horizon” when his play Dutchman appeared on stage off-Broadway. In a way, a few scholars have contended, the play’s theme, a violent encounter between a black man and a white woman in a subway car, represented Baraka’s ultimate break with the downtown denizens, and, if that wasn’t the coup de grace, the assassination of Malcolm X was the final goodbye.

Lula, the white woman in *Dutchman*, perhaps signified and symbolized a world and habits Baraka was seeking to break from, to say nothing of Lula's skinny, white neck. "Shit, you don't have any sense," says Clay, the play's black character. "Nor feelings either. I could murder you now. Such a tiny ugly throat. I could squeeze it flat, and watch you turn blue..."

As Baraka's white character turned blue, Clay became blacker and blacker, rushing madly to the refuge of Black nationalism, hurrying as fast and as tempestuously as he could from Lula's sharp tongue and fatal stab. The transition was just about complete.

Among the more evident signposts of Baraka's move from the Village to Harlem emerges from his poetry. Those seeking the political shifts in his journey to himself would be advised to parse closely his prose, but read even more carefully between the stanzas of his poetic lines. And sometimes you don't have to peer intently because there is no intention to hide behind a simile.

- “We are unfair, and unfair
- We are black magicians, black arts
- we make in black labs of the heart.
- The fair are
- fair, and deathly white
- The day will not save them
- and we own the night.”

This was Baraka’s “state-meant” in 1965 as he irrevocably put intellectual and emotional distance between where he had been and where he was determined to arrive.

Born in New Jersey, Baraka was drawn to Harlem like so many of the other “blues people,” who believed their dreams were on the other side of the cotton curtain, the Gulf of Mexico, the Mississippi River or the Hudson River, as in Baraka’s case. Langston had come from Missouri, Arna Bontemps from California, Wallace Thurman from Utah, Zora from Florida, and Claude McKay from Jamaica, and this was their "heavy Egypt," their pot of gold at rainbow's end. But "Harlem is vicious modernism," Baraka said in one of his poems composed somewhere in the vicinity of 125th Street. But now it was a time for poems "that kill…assassin's poems/poems that shoot guns. Poems that wrestle cops into alleys and take their weapons leaving them dead / with tongues pulled out and sent to Ireland."

Energized by the civil rights movement that by the late sixties and early seventies had morphed into the Black liberation movement, Baraka had found his métier or sinecure—at least for the moment. Now, without reservations and hosannas to Maulana Karenga and his Kawaida philosophy, it was "nation time" for Baraka and his cohorts, all of them genuflecting at the altar of Damballah and Shango. Ancillary to the Black liberation struggle was the Black Arts movement and the always flexible Baraka had that unique ability not only to straddle the artistic and political impulses of the period, but to be a key figure in shaping the strategy and tactics through a succession of organizations, most significantly BARTS (Black Arts Repertory Theater) and CAP (Congress of Afrikan People). But cultural nationalism was just a way station, a stepping stone to a higher, more refined analysis of matter in motion.

His politics, he observed toward the end of this stage of development, was in grave disorder. “Our politics…flowed from our mix-matched and eclectic ideology. We had straight-out white supremacy bourgeois opinions mixed with mass felt revolutionary ones. We wanted to destroy a system and didn’t realize that we still carried a great deal of that system around with us behind our eyes.”

In one of his fugitive essays, Baraka had disavowed Communism, playfully ridiculing the leftist persuasion with the comment that there was no “Marx on his Lenin.” Most of his enemies and even a few of his devoted followers caught wind of his ideological shift in 1974 at the Sixth Pan-African Congress in Dar es Salaam, Tanzania. Delegates from the United States—and they comprised a mish-mash of political tendencies—received copies of Baraka's "manifesto," indicating his new direction: Scientific socialism. At first, many of the delegates presumed it was nothing more than rank opportunism since they were guests in a government where the leader, Julius Nyerere, whose ideas formulated in Ujamaa, bore all the earmarks of socialism.

But the political change—and it was to some extent forecast—was a real one, and Baraka spelled out why it had occurred. "In terms of my change," he declared, "it's based on being involved in struggle—seeing, for instance, the whole nationalist thing turn into its opposite. A lot of people were talking about black liberation, national liberation, and then actually being in charge of the exploitation." What was unmistakably clear to him was that change hadn't occurred and that “skin color was not the determinant of political content.”

The only consistent thing for Baraka was change, though it should be noted that his political oscillations were always in concert with his cultural expression. That is to say, his art reflected his politics and vice-versa. He criticized capitalism and imperialism in his poems with the same fervor he had demonstrated in his political attacks against colonialism and racism in a previous life. “We’ll worship Jesus when mao do/when toure does/when the cross replaces Nkrumah’s star,” he explained in a poem.

For good or bad, Baraka has maintained his communist groove or what some would term “rut.” And the extent to which that may have stifled his artistic growth, I leave to the literary critics to debate. Recently, as we sat in his home while a storm raged outside, (a northerly whiff of Hurricane Gustav) he indicated that while his political activities have toned down a bit, there is no surcease with the writing. Nearby, in a room overburdened with books, are stacks of "Unity & Struggle," his eight-page newsletter where he berates those on the left who, from his vantage point, "lack political clarity" in their denunciation of President elect Sen. Barack Obama. "There are even some utterly backwards cultural nationalist negroes who say 'Obama is their enemy' because he is not demanding that black people stop speaking English and speak their mother tongue (my mother tongue is Afro American) or that he blame the Jews for the world's ills," is the editorial he penned for the paper. "My God! You couldn't win on those planks even if the election was for the NAACP or the Black Panther Party, or the Student Nonviolent Coordinating Committee."

If there was a time in his political maturation that Baraka might have harbored similar notions dismissing Obama, that was ages ago. It's hard to believe that someone who was once adamantly opposed to the impulses of the masses of Black Americans has now adopted a position that follows where the majority of his people are headed. "If 90 percent of the Black people want Obama, what does that tell you?" he asked rhetorically during our interview. "What do you think…that they're just dumb? That they don't know anything and you know something?"

Coaxed back to the realm of literature and asked to comment on certain black writers, particularly Stephen Carter, who we have interviewed and whose work we've reviewed in these pages, Baraka evinced little enthusiasm. "I haven't read anything by him since his first thing on affirmative action was published. That was enough for me, now I hear he's become a novelist. But you shouldn't be surprised in this conservative age we live in. If you're talking about some of the turbulence in the lives of upwardly mobile Negroes, then you can get some play. But if you talk about getting rid of the oppression and right wing ideology, then there's no market for you."

Baraka said he tries to write something everyday. "I have two books coming out this year," he began. "One is called Digging—The Afro-American Soul of American Classical Music. I'm editing this right now. The University of California is the publisher. It's got about ten major essays and seventy other pieces. It's going to be a pretty big book. The other book is called Razor—Revolutionary Art for Culture. This is a collection of pieces on the arts, poetry, literature, et al. Third World Press is publishing it."

He noted that *Home*, his collection of essays of the early sixties, was being reprinted. "I am not that excited about this because I've gone past that and people get confused by where you are," he said.

You would think that a writer of his stature, a writer who once was deemed the rightful heir to the niche left by James Baldwin, and whom, as a young Turk he castigated only to make peace in later years, would have publishers hovering around his door. But he explained that such is not the case, which leaves him with few options, and hardly any attention by the major houses and their sizable advances. “Big advances have not been my legacy,” he lamented. “The main publishing companies where you can get a big advance are controlled by our enemies. You see, I’ve made a name for myself around certain issues and certain ideas and those people don’t want to see them. I know some of these people pretty well, and I know where they’re coming from.”

One option he exercised many years ago during his “narrow nationalist” period was to publish his own works, as well as the works of others. But, he said, that requires too much time, energy and resources, none of which he felt he has in great supply. “I’ve published some of my own books but it’s hard,” he sighed. “We need publishers who can get into print the most advanced things we do, books that begin to tell the truth about this society. So, if you’re looking for the kind of books about truth and candor that James Baldwin wrote, you’re not going to find it. Only the poets are carrying on this mission.”

And Baraka continues to be one of these poets, one of these emissaries who are part visionaries and seemingly always on the cutting edge. Six years ago Baraka’s poetic mission was, to some degree, waylaid when he was asked to resign his appointment as Poet Laureate of New Jersey. He had caused a firestorm of controversy with a poem “Somebody Blew Up America.” His detractors disagreed with Baraka’s conclusion that the poem focused on the domestic terrorism black Americans have endured since slavery times.

At the center of the charges against him—and this was an attack led by the Jewish Anti-Defamation League—was the assertion that his interpretation of the bombing of The World Trade Center was anti-Semitic. Baraka refused to resign despite the pressure from the state.

"This state and indeed this nation and this world," Baraka wrote in a long rejoinder, "is desperately in need of the deepest and most profound human values that poetry can teach. That is what [John] Keats and [W.E.B.] Du Bois called for the poet to do, to bring Truth and Beauty. To be like the most ancient paradigmythic image of the poet. To be like Osiris and Orpheus, whose job it was to raise the sun each morning with song and story. To illuminate the human mind, and bring light into the world."

In our hour long discussion, Baraka opined on a number of subjects, issues and people. For example, here's what he had to say about music critic and social commentator

Stanley Crouch: "I don't think Crouch's book, the one he was supposed to write on Bird [the jazz immortal Charlie Parker], will fill the bebop void left by Max Roach. He has not completed the book and I told him that people was shoving him off in different directions, which wasn't his. Now you're a novelist, now you're a political speaker and he don't know shit about these things. Stanley's most important writing is about music, whether I agree with him or not. He definitely knows something about the music. But when it comes to politics and fiction he has a lack of understanding where we are. Now, he's got our boy [Bill] Cosby picking up on some of his opinions."

He was equally unsparing when it came to assessing the Presidential bid of Cynthia McKinney of Atlanta, who is running on the Green Party ticket. "Some people are going to vote for McKinney because they think they're smarter than the rest of us," he said. "But I think this is some kind of selfish pride. What they are doing in effect is outsmarting themselves. It reminds me of the story where these three guys are sentenced to death. They tried to electrocute the first one who had confessed to murder but the machine didn't work. They tried it with the second one and once more it didn't work. When they prepared the third one for electrocution he said 'You dumb motherfuckers, don't you know you've got to put the red wire with the blue wire?' Well, he left immediately."

When you are in your early seventies as Baraka is, some allowance is given for reminiscing. "Once upon time, back in the sixties," he ruminated, "there were a number of black publications on the market, *the Journal of Black Poetry, Soulbook, Black World, the Black Scholar, Black Books Bulletin, Black Creation,* but that was because of the movement. It's always the people's movement that spurs the other things. When they stop everything sort of cools out.

Just the other day I was looking at a magazine I put out with Larry Neal called Cricket, which was about the music. I would love to see those back in print. And there was Umbra and the Liberator, all of them grew out of the movement. Now all we have is a few slick magazines like Essence and Upscale that are on a wholly different level. The magazines I was talking about earlier were put out by activists, not institutions, like *African American Review*. Those kinds of magazines will have to come back because that's the way we get our story told, and it must be told."

Telling our stories, the American stories, has always been a priority for Baraka, and the latest collection, Tales of the Out & Gone, which copped a PEN Beyond Margins Awards in 2007, is a testament of this resolve. Readers familiar with his work will be reminded of his first volume of short stories, *Tales*, published forty years ago.

Though nowadays a bit physically stooped, Baraka does not stoop to conquer; in fact he remains as fiery today as he was in the sixties when his star blazed incandescently across the political firmament. From LeRoi Jones, roughly "King" Jones to Amiri Baraka or "blessed prince" in Arabic, there may have been a reduction in royalty but he continues to stride leagues ahead and beyond even the younger poets and prophets, and other so-called public intellectuals. He has lost none of that sense of adventure, that Don Quixote audacity, that imaginative vigor, that desire to challenge the state and the status quo.

He expressed a sample of this inextinguishable outrage in a recent letter to Governor Corzine of New Jersey. "I'm writing to register my disgust at a great injustice in this state, in our city of Newark. I am talking about the attempt to remove Central Ward Councilperson, Dana Rone from her office for a minor infraction. Despite a municipal court judge fining Ms. Rone nominally for “interfering with the issuance of a traffic summons” to her nephew, Dana Rone is now faced with being banned from state politics (or from holding any public employment) for life.”

The blessed prince, his pen a trusty lance, will not tolerate even the least harmful dragons among us. And he seems always to meld his artistic vision with his relentless political commitment. He is just as bold and creatively defiant as he was as a student at Howard University when he upset the administration while eating a slice of watermelon in the middle of campus; just as keen to the absurd as he was in those poetical flights in bygone Village nights where he soared with a posse of “angel headed hipsters.”

- “Against what light
- is false what breath sucked, for deadness.
- Murder, the cleansed
- purpose, frail, against

- God, if they bring him
- bleeding, I would not
- forgive, or even call him
- black dada nihilismus."

Who can say what will be the final incarnation as Baraka pursues himself from one terrifying moment to another. It's no easier to speculate where he is bound as to say from what he is fleeing. No matter, whether he is exiting or entering, the benefit will be ours to cherish, even it's nothing more than a warning, a sign outside his home.

Ralph Ellison and the Militants, an essay by Peniel E. Joseph, Ph.D

Ralph Ellison's star crossed relationship with black militants who changed and provocatively challenged America's racial landscape seems almost pre-ordained.

Born in Oklahoma City in 1913, Ralph Waldo Ellison grew up in tragic and humbling circumstances. The death of his father and his mother's perpetually tenuous economic condition made for difficult times. Stubborn, willful and ambitious Ralph managed to enroll at Tuskegee Institute in Alabama with dreams of having a virtuoso music career.

Three years at Tuskegee turned into a detour into the tragic-comic world of black Americans striving for success for success in a world where opportunities where starkly defined by race. Fleeing what he viewed as Tuskegee's intellectual and cultural parochialism, Ellison ventured to Harlem where he would befriend some of the era's leading literary figures, most notably Langston Hughes and Richard Wright.

In Harlem, Ralph soon came under the spell of the Communist Party and the larger interracial left that offered a tantalizingly, if also at times sectarian, cosmopolitan view of the world. Impressed with the literary breakthroughs of William Faulkner and able to imbibe in Wright's pungent prose style, Ellison dreamed of writing a novel so luminous that it would offer unprecedented opportunities to its author.

The result, after a torturous gestation period of nearly a decade, was Invisible Man in 1952. Hailed as a literary masterpiece that transcended racial art for the higher altitudes of genuine literary genius, Invisible Man s 1953 National Book Award cemented Ellison's reputation as perhaps the most important Negro writer of the post-war era.

The publication of a book of essays twelve years later, *Shadow and Act*, furthered Ralph's growing reputation as a cultural critic and essayist. By now in his early middle age, Ellison's former radicalism had evolved into a stubborn embrace of American universalism, despite the racial barriers that still precluded blacks from enjoying the fruits of the nation's democracy. Ellison pursued social and literary connections with powerful white brokers that paid dividends by the late 1960s, when he would be feted as a voice of racial reason amid a searing wilderness of black radicalism.

Cold to younger black writers, Ellison found James Baldwin's stinging critiques of American racism to be distasteful and regarded the fiery young poet LeRoi Jones as a disaster. If Baldwin and Jones unleashed criticism against institutional racism in a bid tomake America more responsive to the needs of the black masses, Ellison (the former radical) now felt that true artists required a bruising self-discipline and technical mastery of craft that forbade entrance into social, historical and political quarrels. Ellison's standoffishness to African decolonization (despite being an avid collector of African art) during the 1950s and early 1960s anticipated his antipathy toward proponents of both the Black Arts and the larger Black Power Movement. As Arnold Rampersad's engaging *Ralph Ellison: A Biography* makes clear, the author of Invisible Man took no prisoners in his belief that racial integration, rather than black separatism, held the key to social justice.

Black Power's notion of a collective African American community particularly rankled Ellison, who took pride by the late 1960s in his laundry list of racial breakthroughs (including election to the American Academy of Arts and Sciences) that were based, he felt, on individual merit rather than race. Comfortable being the only black in largely, at time exclusively, all-white settings, Ellison viewed Black Power's robust nationalism and trumpeting of group solidarity as narrow, clannish, and anti-intellectual.

On this score, he refused the young LeRoi Jones' overtures for support of his ambitious Black Arts Repertory Theater and School that dazzled and scandalized Harlem in the summer of 1965. Though short lived, the Black Arts Movement would soon flourish around thecountry, popping up in the wealth of magazines, journals, and cultural and literary groups devoted to studying the complexity of black life as well as criticizing white America's longstanding refusal to acknowledge it. In this way, the Black Arts Movement represented the cultural arm of Black Power, which promoted radical black self-determination in the service of a social and political revolution

Ironically, the more Ellison purposely distanced himself from the gathering storm of racial protest that enveloped America during the 1960s, the more in demand he was a racial spokesperson. An ardent supporter of the Vietnam War, Ellison stood defiantly out of step with even liberal whites, who increasingly spoke out against the carnage in South East Asia. Ellison's patriotism, unwillingness to support younger black writers, and failure to produce a second novel made him a unique figure; a grand old man of black writers who stood aloof from the growing wave of discontent that, in certain sly instances, Invisible Man had imagined.

As Ellison's fame grew, so did his relative isolation from the black community he had mined so well for his best fiction. He consistently declined invitations to write for most black themed journal and would have a running, mostly one-sided feud, with radical members of the Harlem Writers Guild, such as John Henrik Clarke and John Oliver Killens. In a rare occasion of symmetry, Ellison and Black Power activists, albeit in different settings and tones, decried the "Moynihan Report's" depiction of black pathology centered in a dysfunctional matriarchal familial lineage. Noting that Moynihan looked at black families through "a white cultural pattern," Ellison defended black culture as resilient, disciplined and resourceful. (p. 429)

By 1967, with the summers in America being marked by civil disturbance the government called "riots" and Black Power militants characterized as "rebellions," Ellison agreed to a rare exchange with a group of young black writers published in Harper's. In broad brushstrokes, Ellison painted the Black Arts Movement as bellicose and anti-intellectual. The more Ellison launched invective against black nationalist-based art as nothing more than angry racial Philistinism, the more doors seemed to open up.

Attacked as an Uncle Tom following a panel at Grinnell College, Ellison broke down, crying, "I am not a Tom, I am not a Tom." (p. 440) 1968, the year of the Tet Offensi ve, the assassinations of Martin Luther King, Jr. and Robert Kennedy, May Day rebellions around the world, the trial of Black Panther leader Huey P. Newton, and the election of Richard Nixon, made demand for Ellison swell. As Rampersad puckishly notes, "each terrible event meant, perversely, more prestige and more money for Ralph." (p. 445). Handpicked, lucrative engagements (preferably before integrated audiences) were juxtaposed against Ralph's new ties to worlds of privilege and power. Imploring the tendency of black students to self-segregate during a speech at Brandeis University, Ellison had no qualms about being the sole black on the ever-lengthening lists of boards, philanthropic groups, private clubs and invitation-only social events to which he was becoming ever more accustomed.

Flogged by black writers Ishmael Reed, Amiri Baraka (LeRoi Jones), and Larry Neal as isolated, out of touch, and politically compromised, Ellison remained indefatigably committed to a pluralistic vision of American society that, critics often reminded him, touched the lives of far too few Americans, black or white. For Ellison, Black Power inspired artists "allowed the realities of their social and political situation to determine their conception of their role and freedom as artists." (456).

The sad fact is that Ellison's quarrel with the generation of young writers, poets and artists identified with the Black Arts Movement merely scratched the surface of a deep-grained skepticism of the technical mastery, theoretical sophistication and capacity for genius of black intellectuals. With rare exceptions Ellison's pantheon of gifted writers were white, as were most of the scholars he judged sophisticated enough to analyze his work. These views remained consistent in his personal life as well, where only a privileged few blacks entered the world that he carefully constructed with his wife, Fanny

Baldwin's Harlem: A Conversation with Herb Boyd

By Peniel E. Joseph

I had the pleasure of conducting this interview with Herb Boyd about his latest book *Baldwin's Harlem*. Having written the book's preface, I can attest to the fact that this is one of the most important books produced to date on Baldwin. In many ways Boyd's extensive experience as an author, journalist, and political activist makes him uniquely suited to telling this story.

Peniel Joseph: Why did you decide to write Baldwin's Harlem?

Herb Boyd: As I point out in the book's Preface, this was not my idea. More than half of the eighteen books I've written have been the ideas of others. And they have been very good ideas that I've been blessed to complete, apparently satisfying what they originally envisioned. I guess if I had it my way I'd be writing screenplays and novels, but I've settled quite comfortably in the land of nonfiction and when literary agent Jim Fitzgerald approached me with the idea (we had worked together on Pound for Pound—The life of Sugar Ray Robinson), I leaped on it because Baldwin's books—especially the paperback editions—were the ones I stuffed into my back pocket as a teenager to read whenever I got a chance. The idea to focus the book on Baldwin in Harlem was mine since I had to find an angle on his life that had not been chewed juiceless.

After rereading the bios, I discovered that Baldwin's Harlem period wasn't given a lot of attention, so I decided that it might be worth pursuing that point of view. What finally convinced me that focus on Baldwin's experience in Harlem was a good idea was the completion of the chapter in my book that I call "Harlem—Real and Imagined." I plowed through his literature to see just how he had treated Harlem in his fiction and his nonfiction. Baldwin was both repelled and fascinated by his hometown and only toward the end of his life, particularly in Just Above My Head, was there an extensive look at the community and what it had meant to him.

PJ: Discuss Jimmy Baldwin's special relationship to Harlem?

HB: First of all, he was born in Harlem, and I take some time with the events surrounding his birth in 1924. Most of the opening chapter is devoted to his early years, and being one of nine children, you can imagine the kind of struggle they had surviving on their father's meager income. Nonetheless, Baldwin was an enterprising young man and with his brothers took to the streets to earn money to assist their parents.

Despite the terrible environment, Baldwin managed to find those niches and sinecures of comfort and inspiration. He was exceptionally bright, at least in most subjects, and this brilliance was like a magnet, attracting a cadre of teachers and mentors to rescue him, and to nourish his inquisitiveness. Very early in his life he accepted the circumstances that surrounded him and then sought ways to transcend them, or, to navigate them safely from dawn to sunset.

Throughout his life, I detected a kind of ambivalence, what psychologists might call an approach/avoidance, love/hate relationship. But even after he was able to migrate permanently from Harlem, far too much of it went with him, and this baggage, you might say, is what he grappled with, sometimes imaginatively and sometimes disdainfully.

PJ: Why does Baldwin's story still matter for a contemporary generation?

HB: Baldwin was a witness, not just an ordinary one, but one gifted with a talent to relate what he had witnessed—in the most compelling and eloquent language—and there was something special about his vision, his prophecy. To be blessed with such a mission and the means to fulfill it makes him an exceedingly valuable communicator, no matter what generation discovers his messages. Because he spoke so honestly and passionately to his times—and about the human condition—his words are timeless, and they have universal significance and implications.

And Baldwin was a witness who suffered. Much of his personal and social burden was of his own choosing. He was a saint, who knew he was also a sinner, and he like, all of our great artists, possessed a heavy spirit, one that spoke to us on registers we're still trying to comprehend. One unmistakable and inescapable fact about Baldwin was his ability with words. He was a great writer in the sense that Balzac, Dickens, Twain, and Toni Morrison were and are—and that alone gives him an eternal presence in our world.

PJ: Baldwin was an active supporter of both civil rights and Black Power, but many remain unaware of his enthusiastic assistance of the era's militants. Why did Baldwin defend the Black Panthers, Stokely Carmichael, and Angela Davis?

HB: To defend the underdog, those bereft of hope and possibility, those who suffer the outrageous misfortunes of racism and white supremacy, and sexual and political aggression were candidates for his mercy and support.

Baldwin once wrote that to be a black person in America is to be perpetually in rage. His was a furious passage and he recognized and identified with all the other wretched of the earth. So, in effect, he was not so much coming to the aid of the others in flight or under the gun, he was fighting for his own life, his own salvation. And this salvation was inextricably linked to those he championed, whether in the civil rights movement or Black Power, or the struggle for total liberation, here and abroad.

His mantle of protection extended beyond the militants in America—and he did this at great sacrifice—to the downtrodden of the world, the salt of the earth were deserving of his care and compassion.

PJ: Can you sum up Baldwin's political, social, and literary impact on American society and the larger world? Is this impact continuing to be felt?

HB: There is one certainty about Baldwin, his books will always be in print, at least those that have resonated for readers around the globe—The Fire Next Time, Giovanni's Room, Nobody Knows My Name, and Blues for Mr. Charlie. Recently, I've attended several events in which one of his works has been produced or discussed, or they have provoked seminars, conferences, and other special occasions. He has been adopted by just about every alternative community you can name. Even the hip hop culture is mining his works and just the other day in Compton, California, Sen. Hillary Clinton quoted him—"Those who say it can't be done usually interrupt those who are doing it!" Baldwin was a thorn in the side, ever pricking (and I use that word advisedly) America's conscience, holding up his all-seeing artistic vision to make this nation face its contradictions, to deal with a hypocrisy that has devastated so many dreamers.

Baldwin, at last, was a prophet, and like Dr. King and Malcolm X, he understood his mission, and never wavered from speaking truth to power. "I want to be a great writer," he once wished, and indeed he was—and is.

Call Him Ishmael!

A profile of Ishmael Reed

By Herb Boyd

As a matter of full disclosure, let me say from the jump that any objectivity I might have about Ishmael Reed was wiped out years ago. In 1995, Robert Allen and I received the American Book Award for our anthology, *Brotherman:*

The Odyssey of Black Men in America. That award is given by the Before Columbus Foundation that *jus' grew* from Ishmael's fertile imagination. Though the decision was rendered by the foundation's board, I will always believe that Ishmael had more than a passing nod in our winning that award.

I wonder if Ishmael has ever received an award from the foundation, if not I can't think of any writer—black, white or otherwise—who deserves it more. Of the current crop of prolific black American writers, there is the scholarly Gerald Horne, the intrepid Amiri Baraka, and always busy Molefi Kete Asante, who claims to have written more than 75 books. Ishmael is right up there with these productive wordsmiths, and he, like a Langston Hughes, James Baldwin, Zora Neale Hurston, and James Weldon Johnson of the past, wields a versatility that only Baraka of today can match.

Allen and I cobbled together the creative genius of more than 150 African- American male writers for the anthology, and the piece I selected from Ishmael's vast literary oeuvre was a fragment from *Writin' Is Fightin'*. Sure, I was fascinated by Ishmael's first nationally recognized collection, *19 Necromancers From Now*, and a posse of characters such as Louisiana Red, the Loop Garoo Kid, and such novels as *Yellow Back Radio Brokedown* and *The Free-Lance Pallbearers*, but his essays, over the years, have been equally provocative and full of his typical sass and pizzazz.

That excerpt from *Writin' Is Fightin'* epitomized Ishmael's style and attitude about the literary profession; it also did a wonderful job of providing a bit of autobiography and his first brush with the pen. "In 1953, I was working in a drugstore on William Street in Buffalo, New York," Ishmael wrote. "As I left one evening to go home, a man pulled up to the curb and told me that he needed somebody to help him delivery newspapers. There were stacks of them in the backseat of his old brown beat-up Packard, which was just a shade darker than he was.

"His name was A.J. Smitherman, editor of *The Empire Star Weekly*, a Buffalo newspaper" Ishmael continued. 'How would you like to have this job every week?' he asked after we'd taken copies of the newspaper to all of the newsstands on his route. I had been writing before then, and date my first commissioned work to 1952, when my mother asked me to write a birthday poem for one of her fellow employees at Satler's Department Store on Fillmore."

Since those formative years, Ishmael has compiled an enviable career of letters, and we should note that he has excelled in practically every literary form, most rewardingly I believe in his novels, though here lately he's centered his focus on nonfiction. The evidence of that production stares at me each morning—*Mixing It Up—Taking on the Media Bullies and Other Reflections* and *Barack Obama and Jim Crow Media—The Return of the Nigger Breakers*—beckoning their own reviews, their own opportunity to convince me once again of Ishmael's brilliance, and those unfortunate enough to be his most recent targets, those about to be skewered by his piercing putdowns and wit.

One ongoing, almost inevitable preoccupation for Ishmael is the role of black men in literature and the associated issue of misogyny. I hadn't talked to Ishmael since he was last in New York for a reading at Quincy and Margaret Troupe's salon in Harlem. He was in fine fettle that evening and, unlike his appearance prior to this, the audience didn't get a chance to hear his bebop piano filigree. Those of abiding interest can pick up his CD with his companion Carla Blank on violin. David Murray appears on tenor saxophone.

Anyway, back to misogyny and the imperiled black male writers. When asked about the status of this furious debate he has had with feminists and womanist advocates, Ishmael has never been reticent. "Singling out black men in the United States and Africa to take the blame for world misogyny may not be the mother of all hypocrisies, but maybe the cousin," he wrote in an email. "This theme has made hundreds of millions of dollars for white men in publishing, film, theater, television and the newspaper industry, and some feminists and womanists have behaved as unwitting servants for this enterprise. Not only has this been a huge money maker, but it has muted the strongest American literature of dissent from *Walker's Appeal* (1829) to the writings of Black Panthers, Bobby Seale and Huey Newton. No longer was racism the target of black literature but black men. Men with little power to influence the policies that damage women became the oppressors."

A brutal upshot of this debate with feminists was a charge from Gloria Steinem's *Ms. Magazine* that Ishmael was the worst misogynist in the United States. "I bore the brunt of the misogyny charge," he said, and in his characteristic-fighting mode lashed back at his accusers. "My complaint about this accusation and the hint of a law suit against the white men who ran *Ms.*, at the time, Lang Communications, led to the resignation of Robin Morgan, who was editor at *Ms.* when the article was published."

"Most of the charges against me as a misogynist originate in publications that are owned by white men who are silent about how women are treated in their ethnic group," Ishmael asserted.

" A hit job on my new novel, *Juice!* was done by a critic named Paul Devlin. He objected to my lead character, Paul Blessings, being homophobic and misogynist which is a rule that's not applied to male novelists like Phillip Roth and Saul

Bellow, men who share his background. They want our male characters to sound like Mr. Rogers, or Kermit the Frog. The purpose of this review, which was syndicated, was to drive me out of business. But unlike Richard Wright and Chester Himes, who were silenced when they went too far, I can publish my own books, produce my own CDs and produce my own movies, a lesson I learned when affiliated with the publications *Umbra* and *The East Village Other*, back in the day. This guy Devlin, who works for Skip Gate's *The Root*, where John McWhorter, a proxy for the far right, works, also said that with *Juice!* I had gone 'too far,' which was how slave masters referred to runaway blacks."

Metaphors about slavery and the some of the denizens of the plantation proliferate in Ishmael's literature, and even in the titles such as *Flight to Canada* and *Shovetide in Old New Orleans*. That he has been able to restrain his anger and not resort to stereotypical lacerations of black feminists is commendable, though they are not let off the hook. "Now a few black feminists have attacked me as a misogynist," he lamented, and perhaps none more adamant than the heat he got after his dismissal of the film *Precious.* "But I can't take them seriously because of where their pieces appeared and their contradictions. One hit appeared in *The New Republic*, which is published by Marty Peretz, who said that black women were "culturally deficient."

Margo Jefferson, for many years a mainstay at the *New York Times*, is among those who have taken exception to Ishmael's opinions about gender. "She was so agitated by what she calls my misogyny that she came to a book party I threw for the late Calvin Hernton and was so upset I thought we were going to have to call the police. At a forum held at NYU she challenged me to a fistfight. Yet she wrote that she has erotic fantasies about John Wayne. How can I take someone like that seriously?"

Obviously, we could have devoted this entire profile to his discussion on misogyny but of equal importance to readers and writers is Ishmael's feelings about black male literature. "It has been badmouthed out of the market," he began. "When the great John Wideman has to go to a *vanity press* to get published, it means all of us are in trouble. But kindle, nook and other devices will change that because black men and women who are not into the 'black boogeyman' racket will have access to world markets. Black literature has to go international."

"For example," he explained. "No American publisher would publish my *Barack Obama and The Jim Crow Media, The Return of the Nigger Breakers.* In Canada, where it was published, it's going into a second printing. Hundreds of Africans, Caribbean people, and Afro Americans expats turned out to my book signings in Canada. American critics were too narrowly Eurocentric to understand my *Japanese*

By Spring, but Japanese critics praised it and I got big turnouts when I toured Japan. I was informed on July 16, that interest in *Japanese By Spring* in China has gotten my work declared a national project in that country and there's interest in my coming there."

This Asian breakthrough has given Ishmael further incentive to publish under Ishmael Reed Publishing Company whose editorial director is Carla Blank, their latest tome, *New and Selected Yuri* by Tokyo writer Yuri Kageyama. "Besides the work of Nigerian women we've published, we've added some more American black women to our catalogue including Alison Mills, Kathryn Takara, Karla Brundrige, Neli Moody, and Jerri Lange and the famed Haitian poet, Boadiba. So my advice to younger writers is to go global. As long as they confine themselves to an American audience they will continue to receive blueprints and ultimatums from special interest groups both black and white," he advised. Then, as if to tie the above two themes of misogyny and black male literature together, Ishmael cited one of his colleagues, author Cecil Brown. "In an article he published in *Counterpunch* he said that the charge of black male sexism has been used to undermine literature of black male writers."

Of course, a number of other factors can be added to this equation of erasure.

When you begin a conversation with Ishmael—and I would ask you to check out *Conversations with Ishmael Reed*, edited by Bruce Dick and Amritjit Singh for deeper insight on this profound writer—it's like listening to a majestic concerto, an endless sonata of issues that never fail to resonate with conviction and passion. And since we're on a musical riff, how's the arpeggios and burnished chords nowadays?

"I'm still studying Jazz," he said. "My teacher is the great Jazz pianist, Mary Watkins, who insists that I do my scales and cadences. I'm taking a group into Yoshi's, the San Francisco Jazz club, August, Oct. and Nov. I just had a reel to reel tape of a recording session led by the late bassist, the great Ortiz Walton which I produced in 1970. He was the first black to perform with The Boston Symphony. His sidemen are bassists James Leary and Bill Summers. It's a treasure. I plan to bring out a limited memorial edition."

And what about your talented daughter? "Tennessee and I are running a series I call Midnight Writing During The Day, an answer to Midnight Basketball," he replied. "Timothy, my oldest daughter has completed her second novel. My other daughter, Tennessee and I are running a summer poetry workshops for fifteen black kids. Run a workshop like this and you see the damage that Eurocentrics have done to black children. These are very bright kids, but they have never heard of Richard Wright and more shocking, Ntozake Shange. Black and Hispanic kids are failing in their reading scores because they don't see themselves represented in the cerebral arts. Books by black authors don't get the coverage accorded white authors because the media see sales in presenting blacks as ridiculous or dangerous."

"My novel *Juice!,* illustrated with my drawings," he continued, "has been ignored by the mainstream press because, as my agent said when I began this book, most people believe that O.J. is guilty. That's because he was judged by the media which, as in the Casey Anthony case, keeps judging people as guilty even when a jury has acquitted them."

Despite all his complaints about the world of literature, Ishmael, a winner of the John D. and Catherine T. MacArthur Foundation's "genius grant," confesses that he's doing all right. "I'm doing much better than most black, Hispanic,

Native American, Asian American and white writers who are interested in producing and promoting serious literature," he contends. "I know this. Now, the bloggers have sustained *Juice!* and the most intelligent reviews are coming from that element. Cyberspace will become the rival to the mainstream media that has caused so much damage in the country and can possibly sustain a literature that is despised by some. As a result, the media's coverage of black men is confined to crime and sports; how many black kids know that the head of

NASA or the heads of planetariums in both Philadelphia and New York are black men? How many black kids know that the formula for sending a space shuttle into space and returning it to earth was created by a black woman?

"The representation of blacks, especially black men, that appears in the media daily, amounts to psychological assault. Goebbels would be jealous. Except for a few, black authors aren't part of public education's curriculum. It's time to supplement public education, which has failed not only black and Hispanic kids but white kids as well, with off-campus programs like Midnight Writing. We especially need black and Hispanic male writers to start these programs. They've been kept out of classrooms because of their lack of credentials.

"We have no money. *The Black Repertory Theater* lent us their green room. If some black intellectuals would spend as much energy petitioning for space in their cities for the purpose of setting up Midnight Writing programs as they do making a fetish of the 60s, dozens of summer workshops would be established by now. I challenge Henry Louis Gates who has been appointed Czar of black culture by millionaires, and at least one billionaire, to support Midnight Writing During the Day programs across the country, but he won't."

Anybody out there want to take on the mighty Ish?

On the QT

A profile of poet Quincy Troupe

by Herb Boyd

Quincy Troupe

Okay, quickly.

Who is the Poet

Laureate of the United States?

W.S. Merwin. Very good.

Now, who is the Poet Laureate of New York?

You mean there is one?

How about Harlem?

Wasn't that Langston Hughes?

For all intents and purposes, but never in an official way, Hughes was the Poet Laureate of Harlem. But there is a small coterie of literati, the cognoscenti of letters who insist that Quincy Troupe would be a nice choice today.

Indeed. And particularly so when you take a gander at his resume, his published works, his teaching creds, and his impressive track record as a "C.C. Writer," the C.C. in this case being the cultural circuit.

"I just got back from San Francisco where I received the Before the Columbus Foundation Lifetime Achievement Award," he said to me recently. Each year writers are selected in a number of various categories for the American Book Award, which he has won on two occasions. He noted that his longtime friend and colleague, Amiri Baraka wasn't there to receive his award for nonfiction.

"It was a splendid occasion and I spent some time with Ishmael Reed," Troupe continued. Reed, the prolific writer, musician, and unbridled public intellectual, is largely the founder of the Foundation.

Before the trip to the coast, Troupe was in the Motor City for a reading.

"It was a very good reading and turnout, and Detroit shows some signs of getting back where it used to be as a culture capital."

Very few poets and writers can match Troupe's versatility or energy on the literary ramparts. Once I asked him how many readings he did a year and he said it was so many that he lost count. Like the best studio musician who is always in demand, Troupe stays on the road it seems. Whether in clubs in front of musicians—and he knows practically all of the major players—in the academic realm from high school to college, or at conferences, seminars, or wherever folks gather for fine literature, he's a consistently powerful presence.

Troupe also has a knack of being in the right place at the right time, especially from the standpoint of being a witness at a historic moment in our culture. When Miles Davis was looking for someone to collaborate with him on his autobiography, Troupe was ready and willing, and those of you who have had the good fortune of reading *Miles: The Autobiography*, you know what a challenge it must have been to work with someone as singularly unique and iconic as Miles Davis.

One of the most memorable moments in Troupe's life—and it's not easy to single out one—was his interview with James Baldwin, who was virtually on his deathbed. That interview and other times with Baldwin formed the centerpiece of his collection of essays on the great writer's life: *James Baldwin: The Legacy*. A number of authors, teachers and scholars have found that work indispensable in gaining a better understanding of Baldwin's furious passage.

Most recently Troupe held forth at the annual Charlie Parker Jazz Festival at Marcus Garvey Park in Harlem. No, he wasn't reading. He was there to hear the music but was soon cornered by several well-wishers seeking his impressions on sundry social and political issues. He regaled them with intimate stories about Davis, Baldwin, and a gaggle of personalities he has encountered since leaving

California and the Watts Workshop, and even before while a student at Grambling.

"Miles was a, well, you know the rest, if you've read his book," Troupe said, choosing not to mention Davis's favorite expletive. "But I relished every moment in his company. He was a genius, and he loved Jimmy Baldwin."

Among the things that made his relationship with Davis so fruitful—and it may become even more fruitful if the film project on the trumpeter's life is finished with Troupe's pen guiding the way—is that he and Davis both originated from the environs of St. Louis. That commonality served Troupe well when he began to grapple with the awesome task of framing Davis's legendary trajectory, including the drugs, the women, and the phenomenal musicians under his tutelage and spell.

Plus, given his size and attitude, Davis wasn't able to intimidate him like he had done to so many others who dared to get too close. "I was able to deal with him on his own terms without compromising one bit of my integrity or the project I was assigned to complete," Troupe once told a reporter.

Troupe's size, something he inherited from his father who was a Negro Baseball League Hall of Fame catcher and one of a few to handle Satchel Paige's fast ball and curves, was of great advantage during his years at Grambling where he starred on the basketball court just before Willis Reed arrived, who later became a favorite of New York Knicks fans.

But sports couldn't compete with his desire to become a writer, and the stint with Budd Schulberg and the Watts Writers' Workshop was the impetus he needed to propel his emerging career.

My own affiliation with him began in the 1970s when Troupe's pad in Manhattan was the place to be. On any given evening you might run into Hugh Masekela or his sister, Barbara, the noted literary agent Marie Brown, Clyde Taylor, or many of the other notables who continue to congregate around *Black Renaissance Noire*, the publication he currently edits.

Back in those days his fabulous collection of essays, poetry and fiction contained in *Giant Talk* was the talk of the town, and it continues to claim a very special place for those interested in a variety of ideas from a diverse international ensemble of thinkers. And toward the end of the late seventies when *Roots* was thing, Troupe was approached by David Wolper, who produced the television series on Alex Haley's epic family saga, who contracted him to write a book about the impact of the series on the world.

When asked about the cultural scene in Harlem today, Troupe was immediately expansive and expressive, noting that all the rumors about a "Second Harlem Renaissance" may be still born if something more isn't done to promote it. "There are probably more places to hear the music, poetry, and discuss art than there was in the in the 1920s when Langston and Zora were on the scene," he observes, "but you'll never know about it because the media is not interested. They are preoccupied with violence, death and destruction. In other words, as they say, if it bleeds it leads."

Troupe, who lives in Graham Court in the heart of Harlem with his wife, Margaret, and where they host and promote book-signings and artistic performances-- ticks off a list of sites in and around Harlem where there is a prevalence of culture on display. "St. Nick's Pub, Margie Elliott's place uptown for Sunday jam sessions, Lenox Lounge, George

Preston's art gallery and George Faison's Firehouse are just a few places that come quickly to mind," he said.

His own place should be on the list as well, except when he and his wife are recharging their seemingly inexhaustible batteries on the French Caribbean island of Guadeloupe.

But back to the idea of a poet laureate, which is topic that Troupe has some familiarity with since he once occupied such a notch of prestige in California.

Over the last decade or so, there have been at least two people claiming to be Deputy Mayor's of Harlem. These are just claims and such positions may never be. However, a Poet Laureate of Harlem is not just a fancy title or a pipedream; it's a plateau and honor a community of Harlem's stature and acclaim should have. And who should it be?

Well, Quincy Troupe would be a worthy candidate.

Look at these bona fides: His latest books of poetry are *The Architecture of Language*, published in 2006; *Transcircularies: New and Selected Poems*, published in 2002, and selected by Publishers Weekly as one of the 10 best books of poetry published in that year; *Miles and Me*, published in 2000, a memoir of Miles Davis, and *The Pursuit of Happyness*, co-authored with Chris Gardner and published in 2006, which the motion picture is based upon

Moreover, check this out from one of his earlier books *Weather Reports*:

Eighth Avenue Poem, Uptown

on eighth avenue

uptown, in black harlem,

between 116th & 121

streets, on corners

some of the junkies

have shot so much smack

into the soles of their feet

they could step on a dime

& tell you whether

it was heads, or tails

Nuff said.

John Oliver Killens—A Life of Black Literary Activism

By Keith Gilyard

Reviewed by Herb Boyd

Only the most unenlightened, totally distracted participant at the Tenth National Black Writers' Conference at Medgar

Evers College this year missed the significance of the late John Oliver Killens (1916-1987) and his tireless dedication at the event's very inception, in 1986. In fact, the subtitle of the bi-annual conference was And then We Heard the Thunder: Black Writers Reconstructing Memories and Lighting the Way.

Killens' legacy was invoked at practically every panel, where his literary genius, whether as a novelist, essayist, critic, polemicist, anthologist, or political activist, was roundly praised.

And for those who missed the panels, there were copies of the Killens Review of Arts & Letters, edited by Fred Beauford with a brief but poignant profile of Killens by Dr. Brenda Greene, executive director of the Center for Black Literature.

Keith Gilyard, in his absolutely absorbing biography of Killens' literary activism, wasn't able to include his assessment of this most recent gathering, but he assiduously captures nearly every important moment of Killens' highly productive life. In an almost diary-like manner, Gilyard painstakingly tracks Killens' remarkable odyssey, and if he missed a meeting or conference where Killens held forth, only his family, including his son-in-law the poet Louis Reyes Rivera, would know.

Gilyard shadows Killens' journey with deft precision and in doing so brings into sharp relief the times in which he lived, those who influenced him and the thousands he influenced.

Most literary hounds know of Killens from his novels, and none more notable than And Then We Heard the Thunder, which Gilyard, as he does with each of the author's books, carefully and thoughtfully limns. The same meticulous concern is given to the various lectures, essays, seminars, and conferences where Killens' insight is center stage. To accomplish this with such diligence and accuracy means

Gilyard is either a determined collator or had the complete cooperation of the family and their archival supply of Killens' papers.

Whatever the case, the book is a fantastic testament to a writer and activist who was as unstinting in his literary pursuits as he was uncompromising in his political stances. One of the most engrossing chapters in the book is Gilyard's discussion of Killens' position on the race/class dichotomy that created so much turmoil and dissension among black activists in the mid-seventies.

As Gilyard observes, Killens was not a Johnny-Come-Lately to political infighting, particularly between those who professed that the principal contradiction in the struggle to overthrow the oppressor was class and those who posited race as the fundamental problem. "…I insist that the Black question is both a class question and a race question," Gilyard writes, quoting Killens. "One can be both a Pan

African nationalist and at the same time be an advocate of socialism."

Killens was able to take this middling position because he had walked and talked to the likes of Paul Robeson, W.E.B. Du Bois, Harry Haywood, Howard "Stretch" Johnson, and other Marxist thinkers. And he knew well the sympathies and objectives of the nationalist such as Haki Madhubuti, who early on helped Killens shape the conferences that gave his name a lasting legacy.

Killens saw the strengths and weaknesses of both proponents and chose not to side with either the "narrow nationalists" or the "mechanical Marxists."

While much of the biography charts Killens' life in a praiseworthy way, there are moments when Gilyard is critical of the subject's production. He is not afraid to note some of the Killens' shortcomings, especially in the unpublished The

Minister Primarily, which he views as “overdrawn and a bit suffocating.” Even so, he adds, Killens’ humor bursts through and the manuscript is to some degree redeemed.

But if Killens had done no more than organize the Harlem Writers Guild, along with the esteemed John Henrik Clarke, his place in the pantheon of black literature would be secure. A host of writers profited from the Guild—Maya Angelou, Sarah Wright, Rosa Guy, Ossie Davis, Ruby Dee, and countless others.

Film buffs will be interested to read Gilyard’s examination of *Odds Against Tomorrow*, the film starring Harry Belafonte; for many years people were under the impression that Killens had authored the screenplay. Gilyard gets to the bottom of this affair, explaining that while Killens was not the author, he played a decisive role in restructuring the film’s ending.

Gilyard does a fair job of dealing with the derogations and attacks on Killens by Harold Cruse, whom he concluded, “had read little” of Killens’ writings and “certainly none of it closely.” But to Killens, Cruse was nothing more than a “literary hatchet man,” and chose not to waste a lot of time and energy challenging his vindictiveness. He would, however, expend more than a passing nod to William Styron and his novel The Confessions of Nat Turner, in which the author offers his “meditations on history.” To Killens, the book was nothing more than a “fake illusion of reality because it legitimatized all of their [white Americans] myths and prejudices about the American black man…”

In the end, Gilyard has performed an admirable service and it’s hard to believe anyone will be more definitive in capturing the wide arc that Killens cut through the literary firmament. And while the book’s length is satisfactory, with twelve pages of photos and an extensive bibliography, an index would have given it additional value.

I don't think Gilyard will mind if we give Killens the last word: "Don't write about the Negro," he advised his young protégés. "But surely the American Negro is the most uniquely American of all Americans, because he was created here, in this place, physically, psychologically, sociologically, culturally, and economically. He is an American product. The Negro, in his black presence, is the barometer of the nation's Constitution, and all its democratic traditions yet realized." And John Oliver Killens was emblematic of this essence.

A Very Brief History With the Talented Mister Marlon James

A Profile by Herb Boyd

Marlon James

One evening last September, after getting off the A-Train in Harlem, as I walked toward the exit at 145th Street, I noticed a young man with dreads sitting on a bench, presumably waiting for the next train. What caught my eye was a Strand shopping bag beside him overflowing with books.

A black man with books, particularly a bunch of them from my favorite bookstore in New York City, warranted more than a passing glance. Furthermore, he looked familiar.

The closer I got to him the more familiar he looked. Why it was the author Marlon James!

I was stunned to see him sitting there like any one of the homeless folks who frequent the station. I had met him for the first time a week or two before when we were panelists at the Brooklyn Book Festival in 2014.

In fact, he was the moderator, and it didn't appear to be his *métier* since the topic was of non-fiction with Greg Grandin, an expert on the works of Herman Melville, and I as the discussants. Even so, he held his own with probing questions about Melville and Malcolm X.

Before that event I had heard of Marlon from a friend,

Kurt Thometz, an antiquarian with a bookstore in Upper Manhattan. The bookstore was on the bottom floor of his brownstone and in the back he had a room, a bed and breakfast unit that Marlon often used whenever he was in town.

After the panel we promised to stay in touch, but I knew that was just small talk, so, we bade each other farewell and went our separate ways.

So, you can imagine my amazement to see him in the subway, hunched over a book, waiting for a train.

I greeted him and at first he seemed puzzled, trying to figure out who I was. His recognition of me did not arrive fast enough, so, I reminded him of our shared Brooklyn event. There was a brief smile, a kindly nod, and I realized that I was an intruder who was interrupting his reading.

Kurt had told me that he was a voracious reader and, when he wasn't reading, he was busy working nonstop on one of his books. I had read none of his books. In fact, but for his praise, I may not have ever paid them attention.

Given his overwhelming raves, I decided I would get his latest book *A Brief History of Seven Killings,* (Riverhead Books, 2014). I got it on my Nook from Barnes and Noble and, since I was in the process of completing my own book and preparing to teach my class at the City College of New York, began reading it intermittently.

Always, in the spring, when I teach a course on "The History of Harlem," I take my students on a tour of the community. One of the stops on the tour is Kurt's erstwhile bookstore, where they are permitted to browse his vast collection and purchase a book or two, if they so desire.

Kurt is a raconteur and storyteller of the highest order—he can beguile and mesmerize any group of students. Last spring I took the students there when Marlon happened to be in town, on a temporary break from his teaching duties at

Macalester College in St. Paul, Minnesota.

He came in the middle of Kurt's presentation, sat for a moment and then scurried to the back of the store to his room.

Later, after Kurt had finished and the students were preparing to depart, Marlon came from the back and, so it appeared, sat down to chat.

He's not a great talker, especially not with strangers, so, getting him to discuss his writing is challenging. Having read portions of his lengthy novel—it's more than 680 pages—I wanted him to expound on some of the characters in the book, many of them hitmen assigned to kill a character he calls "The Singer," obviously, the great reggae musician Bob Marley.

Here's a short passage from *A Brief History of Seven Killings* about Demus, one of the potential hit men.

"Me is a wicked man, me is a sick man," Demus

confesses to his solicitor in the heavy Jamaican dialect that populates the book, “but me would never join in this if I did know that he want to rub out the Singer. This hurt me brain worse than anything ever hurt me before. All me now don’t sleep. I lie in my room with my eye wide open hearing me girl snore in her sleep.”

Perhaps I should take a moment here to contextualize Demus’s dilemma. In 1976, Marley was wounded by gunmen who invaded his home in Kingston, Jamaica. His wife, Rita, and his manager, Don Taylor, were also seriously wounded.

Despite his wounds, Marley performed at the planned concert two days later. It would be two years before Marley set foot again in his home country. Marlon uses this incident as the central theme of his book, while delivering a boatload of history and information on gangs, violence, language, and politics.

Demus is just one of more than 75 characters Marlon summons, many of whom are based on actual people, though most are composite figures. Whether real or imagined, most have full chapters devoted to them and their intentions.

***

At the Brooklyn Book Festival, where he was a main presenter, he had another obligation. He gave a lively discourse on the prevalence of violence in *A Brief History of Seven Killings*. As the title suggests, hardly a page is turned that isn't chocked with some sort of violence or murder.

During our moments together, there wasn't much time to talk about the creative process, though he did make it clear about how much time and research went into each of his books.

As for the violence, he has explained that in several interviews, "I didn't want to fall into a pornography of violence but I think violence should be violent." On that the reader is not shortchanged.

A Brief History of Seven Killings is by no means brief nor is it an easy read. Not only is the length intimidating but the Jamaican lingo is sure to leave many readers bewildered. Even so, Marlon has filled this epic story with so much intrigue and brio that you are soon swept up in it, willing to sail along with a raft of thugs with nothing but larceny and murder on their minds.

During one session with Kurt and another colleague George Preston, a noted Africanist and curator, I listened as they rhapsodized about the book, dissecting characters, grappling with the convoluted plot, and expressing unabashed exuberance over the sizzling passages of imagery.

Clearly, they're not alone in their enthusiasm for the book. When Michiko Kuakutani of the *New York Times* can drop heavy praise on the novel, it's almost equivalent to Oprah Winfrey's stamp of approval.

"It's like a [Quentin] Tarantino remake of *The Harder They Come* but with a soundtrack by Bob Marley and a script by Oliver Stone and William Faulkner, with maybe a little creative boost from some primo *ganja*," Kukutani wrote in one of her more illuminating paragraphs. "It's epic in every sense of that word: sweeping, mythic, over-the-top, colossal and dizzyingly complex. It's also raw, dense, violent, scalding, darkly comic, exhilarating and exhausting — a testament to Mr. James's vaulting ambition and prodigious talent."

To this literary brew mix in a little Doctorow and Jimmy Cliff and some Tarantino mayhem and you're partially there.

And from whence has sprung this prodigious talent? Well, Marlon was born in Kingston, Jamaica, in 1970, so he was a mere tot when Marley was negotiating a *détente* between Michael Manley and Edward Seaga, two political candidates for Jamaica's leadership (who figure so prominently in the novel.)

He earned a degree in literature from the University of the West Indies in 1991 and a master's in creative writing from Wilkes University in Pennsylvania in 2006. *John Crow's Devil*, his first novel published in 2005, anticipates the latest one in its setting in Jamaica, where there is a spiritual contest between religious rivals. Though American readers will find it hard not to think of Jim Crow. Four years later he published *The Book of Night Women*, and again the number seven is invoked, only this time they are slave women plotting a rebellion.

John Crow is mentioned in connection with Demus toward the end of the book, when he is being hunted by Rastas. Demus was left "swinging from a tree in the John Crow Mountains, the john-crows already gone with his eyes and lips." Eventually, nearly all the hitmen and foot-soldiers suffer a similar fate, though they failed to exterminate "The Singer." (Marley died of brain cancer on May 11, 1981, in the Cedars of Lebanon Hospital in Miami.)

Marlon is the product of middle class family—his mother was a detective and his father a lawyer—but there is little about him that radiates such a privileged background. It was a household with dinner talk that must have rubbed off on the fervid imagination of young Marlon. He dresses in black leather, his left ear adorned with a ring, and he walks with a quick pace, his dreads flapping across his well-developed shoulders.

I was surprised to learn he is gay, a fact he disclosed in a "coming out" piece in the *New York Times*. In this long confessional, he recalled his anxiety with his homosexuality and thought seriously of suicide.

Homophobia in Jamaica, according to a recent study, is

almost as pervasive as hemp.

"At 28 years old, seven years out of college," Marlon wrote, "I was so convinced that my voice outed me as a fag that I had stopped speaking to people I didn't know. The silence left a mark, threw my whole body into a slouch, with a concave chest, as if trying to absorb impact. I'd spent seven years in an all-boys school: 2,000 adolescents in the same khaki uniforms, striking hunting poses, stalking lunchrooms, classrooms, changing rooms, looking for boys who didn't fit in. I bought myself protection by cursing, locking my lisp behind gritted teeth, folding away my limp wrist and drawing 36-double-D girls for art class. I took a copy of *Penthouse* to school to score cool points, but the other boys called me 'batty boy' anyway — every day, five days a week. To save my older, cooler brother, I pretended we weren't related. At home, I lost myself in Dickens's London, Huck Finn's Mississippi River or Professor Xavier's

School for Gifted Youngsters. One day after school, instead of going home, I walked for miles, all the way down to Kingston Harbor. I stopped right at the edge of the dock, thinking next time I would just keep walking."

Rather than keep walking, he kept writing. And to some degree that homosexuality took a creative turn in *A Brief History of Seven Killings* through the Weeper's narrative though Marlon has disputed any connection between him and the character. Some of Marlon's most vividly seductive writing unfolds around one of the Weeper's sexual episodes. Witness this one: "He back in my mouth before I can say, bad man don't kiss. Sucking my tongue, moving his lips over my lips, tongue on tongue, dancing it and making me do it back. He is making me think like a faggot."

I wondered if any of those distressing critical moments circled back on him when he heard he had won the Man Booker Prize, among the most prestigious and richest of his many awards.

I fired off an email to him, but, knowing, Marlon, I expected no response. (I did hear from Ta-Nehisi Coates after he read my review of his book *Between the World and Me*, and, like Marlon, he's flying high, and, taken together, they should be inspiration for a number of struggling black male writers. See Robert Fleming's essay in these pages.)

So, the young man I saw bent over a book on the subway, was now the darling of the literary world, and rolling in dough. The interviews rained on him like the fusillade of bullets intended for Marley's body.

Now, rather than the Levi's and loose shirts hanging outside his tight pants, he was sporting a tux with a bowtie, holding aloft his treasured prize.

There's also a photo of him with Kurt's cat in the *The New York Review of Books*, something I learned from Kurt, after asking if he had heard from the esteemed author.

“I hear from him all the time,” he related in a phone conversation. “In fact, they just had a Marlon James Day in Minnesota.”

The whole state?

“Yes, the entire state,” he said. “And, from Facebook I saw where he was in Brazil.”

Marlon is riding an incredible crest of adulation and celebrity, the kind of sabbatical he probably never dreamed of.

But there’s little time for dreaming for a writer in demand, and it’s reported that he’s in the midst of completing a project for HBO. If it’s a dramatization of his novel, then the network’s viewers are in for a treat that will have all the makings of “The Wire” and “The Sopranos” with an undulating reggae soundtrack.

Harlem Renaissance: Five Novels of the 1920s
Edited by Rafia Zafar

The Library of America | 867 pages | $35.00

Reviewed by Loretta H. Campbell

Neither Black Nor Proud

"My color shrouds me in..." (from "The Shroud of Color," a poem by Countee Cullen) is in the foreword to Wallace Thurman's novel, *The Blacker the Berry.* If being black is a living death, then being dark skinned is the hell that comes after death, according to this work. The book exposes one of the most traumatizing secrets of the African Diaspora—colorism. Tragically, this pigmentation fixation is the only disease/remnant of slavery that is fully embraced and often celebrated by people of African descent around the world. It is a known fact that Thurman himself battled his peers in the Harlem Renaissance because of their insistence that the light-skinned should lead the race.

The heroine of the novel, Emma Lou, is dark-skinned. Her father Joe Morgan was dark-skinned and abandoned his wife and child during Emma Lou's infancy. Thurman intimates that Joe did so to escape the prejudice of his spouse and her family. The girl's mother clearly has no affection for Emma Lou.

"She had been certain that it [the baby] would be a luscious admixture, a golden brown with all its mother's desirable facial features and its mother's hair. But she hadn't reckoned with nature's perversity…" The mother often hid her daughter away when company came to visit.

Because Emma Lou comes from a middle-class background, she never wants for material comforts. However, her relatives shun her, and she has no friends in her home town. Despite the emotional lack in her life, she excels in school and goes away to college.

Here Thurman excoriates the infected "blue vein" policy of so many black sororities. When neither Emma Lou nor her one college friend Grace, also dark-skinned, is pledged for a sorority, Grace explains, "Because you are not high brown or half white." The "half white" specification is significant. The book outlines how important it was to many descendants of slaves to whiten up the race. The closer they were to looking like "massa," the better they were as human beings, they proclaimed.

Emma Lou's journey to self-acceptance leads her to Harlem and eventually a career. It also leads her to more emotional abuse and masochism. In many ways, this book is autobiographical. Thurman was dark-skinned and very likely suffered the same bigotry as his novel's character.

Yet there is a fearlessness in this book that is completely absent in the other four of the volume. Thurman lets the secret out. Though all of these books are well written, none of them takes that step. In fact, three of them bemoan the fate of the tragic mulatto.

In her novel, *Quicksand*, Nella Larsen sees two classes of Black people. There is the 5% of light-skinned ones. These are the ones with innate privileges and recent white ancestors. Then there are the darker ones. They can neither pass nor make a living, according to Helga Crane, the novel's protagonist. Helga is the daughter of a white mother and a black father. She has definite opinions about the way black women should dress. "Bright colors are vulgar"---"Black, gray, brown, and navy blue are the most becoming colors for colored"—"Dark complected people shouldn't wear yellow, or green or red."

We meet her as she is deciding to leave her job as a teacher in an all-black college in the South. The college, in her experience, simply serves to teach Black people to accept the injustice of racism. Because she has no intention of supporting the school's legacy, she quits. However, Helga is not as concerned with the treatment of the students as she is with having a life of ease and beauty, or so she says.

On the train to Chicago, she describes in sickening detail the Jim Crow of public transportation. "A man, a white man, strode through the packed car and spat twice, once in the exact centre of the dingy door panel, and once into the receptacle which held the drinking water." The author doesn't bother to say that the conductor did nothing about this. There is mention of the filth on the floor and the decrepit seats. Helga begs for and gets a sleeping compartment away from the filth and the other black people.

From this point on, Larsen builds the reasons for Helga's need to escape into white society. Helga comes into some money, and soon after, she moves to Denmark to live with her white relatives.

"This, then, was where she belonged. This was her proper setting. She felt consoled at last for the spiritual wounds of the past." Larsen lets Helga and the reader live in this fantasy world for a little while. Then there is a harsh but predictable reality. The story's title has a stinging irony at its conclusion.

The paradox of *Plum Bum,* written by Jessie Redmon Fauset, revolves around a long-suffering "mulatto" named Angela Murray. Angela is light-skinned enough to be mistaken for white and begins passing as one as a child. Although she is often exposed for doing this, she continues. As an adult, she is determined to make a living as a painter.

She sees whiteness as a passport to fame and fortune in her chosen career. For a time, she is correct. Once Angela meets a wealthy white man, she shuns her darker skinned sister.

“I beg your pardon, but isn’t this Mrs. Henrietta Jones?”…Really you have the advantage of me. No. I’m not Mrs. Jones.” The denial traumatizes the younger sister, and dehumanizes Angela.

It is almost fitting that the new boyfriend is a racist who has black people thrown out of restaurants. He goes into rants about the “darkies” who leave the South in search of jobs and social equality. In his view, which he expresses to Angela regularly, Black folks have one place—under the heel of people like him.

It becomes obvious that he would kill Angela if he found out she’s black. Fauset shies away from this revelation, however. As a result, the story lacks depth. She describes her book as “a novel without a moral.” That might not be true. The moral seems to be pass if you can, as soon as you can.

There is no interest in subterfuge in Claude McKay's *Home to Harlem*.Jake, the novel's protagonist, is a working class Black man who is proud of who he is. Stationed in Europe during WWI, he deserts the army because he doesn't like the way black soldiers are discriminated against. From there he (like all the protagonists in this volume) ends up in Harlem.

“Harlem for mine!” cried Jake. “I was crazy thinkin' I was happy over heah. …O, boy! Harlem for mine!”

McKay's use of slang and dialect makes the novel vibrant and realistic. His Harlem has nightclubs and after-hours joints. There are dice players, whores, pimps, and violence. Jazz babies rule. Yet McKay makes some serious political points.

When Jake is asked to be a scab during a strike of a predominantly white union, he explains why he refuses: "Nope, I won't scab, but I ain't a joiner kind of fellah." Still Jake knows that racism is alive and well in unions too. "When I longshored in Philly I was a good union man. But when I made New York I done finds out that they gived the colored mens the worser piers and holds the bes'n a them foh the Irishmen."

Unlike the other characters in these novels, Jake is not judgmental. He is upfront in his views and his friends include gay and straight, criminal and non-criminal, the literate and the illiterate.

Throughout the novel, he is looking for a woman that he had a brief liaison with. He doesn't know her name, but he's sure he'll find her again in Harlem. He lives by his own set of ethics. Though his friends try to encourage him to be kept by women, Jake refuses to let a woman support him. He never criticizes his friends for doing drugs. His motto is he'll try any drug once, and once only.

By all accounts, the grittiness of the book offended McKay's peers. They thought he degraded Black folks by depicting the ugly side of (their) perfect Harlem.

Without fear or favor, Jean Toomer's novel *Cane*offers several vignettes on Black life. The work includes poems, stream of consciousness pieces, and short stories. Here too, is violence. White men kidnap and rape black women and insanity abounds.

In one story, "Box Seat," a man seems deeply constrained while pursuing the woman he loves. Toomer implies that her refusal of him leads him to what is either a psychotic break or a religious experience during a Sunday worship service.

"JESUS WAS ONCE A LEPER?" he shouts. The man's behavior is so frightening that the woman can't wait to get away from him.

The word *cane* appears numerous times throughout this book. It becomes a symbol of Black people continually being cut, broken, or consumed.

The theme of complexion prejudice is repeated here, too. In "Bona and Paul," college students go on a double date. The dark-skinned black man seems to be modeled on Paul Robeson. He is bright, an accomplished athlete and a natural leader. Unfortunately, he doesn't understand the flirting cues of his girlfriend.

More than hints are dropped in the tragic "Blood-Burning Moon." This is the nightmare story of a black woman spurning the advances of a white man in a southern town.

Toomer covers a lot of territory in *Cane*. He touches on racism, sexism, and anti-Semitism. The poems are existentialistic while the short stories are hard-hitting and earthy.

It's as if he's leading the reader through a penny arcade, inviting a brief glimpse at sights on either side of the aisle.

In some ways that is what this volume does. All of the writers examine the collective psyche of Black people. Admittedly, this huge unlimited consciousness has been warped and shaped by slavery, racism, and colorism. All of these isms, though not as present as they were in the 1920s, still inform our lives.

When major pop stars destroy their skin and hair to appear white, something has gone horribly wrong in the

Black community. In some ways, Black people in the 21st century still see their skin as grave clothes, as Cullen suggests. Only now, with the new technology, we bleach out the color and are "reborn" as white.

Harlem Renaissance Four Novels of the 1930s

The Library of America Collection

Edited by Rafia Zafar

Reviewed by Loretta H. Campbell

New Beginnings

"**S**uddenly the aged Negro dropped to one knee, his hands resting on the arm of the planter's [master's] chair, and began weeping aloud." This is a passage from *Black Thunder,* by Arna Bontemps, and one of the four novels in this extraordinary volume, a companion to *Harlem*

Renaissance Five Novels of the 1920s, also edited by Rafia Zafar(author of *We Wear the Masks).*

In this section, Ben, a house slave in southeastern Virginia during the 1800s, betrays a slave insurrection, condemning hundreds of his brothers and sisters to horrible deaths.

Bontemps describes Ben as the aged house slave/butler who believed his master's life and comfort were more valuable than the lives of Ben's own people. In short, Ben was exactly as his master described him, "a good boy."

Unfortunately, the leaders of the insurrection believed that Ben and another slave were trustworthy. Bontemps gives us an intimate portrait of Ben's mindset and that of the leaders of the aborted insurrection.

"Don't you want to be free, fool," Blue said.

"I reckon I does."

"You *reckon*?"

Bontemps, one of the stars of the Harlem Renaissance, culled thousands of slave narratives before he found this particular slave revolt.

According to the notes in the back of this volume, he used the renowned Fisk University Library for his research. Bontemps combined fact and fiction in this novel. Unlike the more famous slave insurrections, this one terrified the whites in Virginia and across the southeast. Apparently, it aroused their deepest fears of being outnumbered by angry slaves. In fact, according to Bontemps, slaves were in the majority in that part of Virginia at the time. The leaders of the attempted insurrection organized virtually in full view of the slavers. Their planning was flawless and completely undetected.

During his trial, the designated general, Gabriel, explained to the prosecuting attorney how the slaves were going to take over the territory.

"…and how did you imagine you'd be able to take the city?"

"We was ready to hit fast. We had three lines, and the one in the middle was going to split in two. They was coming in town from both ends at once. They wasn't going to spare nothing what helt up its hand against us."

The town contained an arsenal and ammunition. The slaves were poised to take it and liberate their brothers and sisters as far south as they could.

A master of metaphor, Bontemps explains the fate that Ben can expect at the hands of his fellow slaves by the end of the novel.

"But Ben could not forget Gabriel's shining naked body or the arc inscribed by the executioner's ax. He could not feel reassured about the knives that waited for him with the sweet brown thrashers in every hedge and clump."

House slaves of a different sort are the focus of George S. Schuyler's scathing satire, *Black No More*. In this book, the black people don't want to please massa. They want to *be* massa. As the title suggests, Blackness becomes a thing of the past. A new scientific treatment turns black people into white people, complete with straight blonde hair. In no time, Black people disappear, and the majority of America's inhabitants are white.

Schuyler pours a kind of sulfuric acid on the characters of the book that are clearly drawn from real-life notables. Their names are suggestive of their personalities. One of the senators is named The Honorable Walter Brybe. The black doctor who administers the treatment is named Dr. Junius Crookman.

Representatives of the NAACP, labor unions, the Black church, the Ku Klux Klan, and senators of dubious ancestry want the treatment outlawed. The leaders of Black America would be out of jobs if there was no racism. The KKK doesn't want white America sullied by Blacks passing for white. Racists unions don't want Black laborers competing for their jobs. With the new treatment, there's no way to parcel out the jobs to a chosen few whites. Some of the senators themselves have been passing for white for years. This new treatment is causing Americans to question the ancestry of even their trusted elected officials.

Schuyler takes his annihilating and irreverent humor to the next level. The protagonist, a hustler named Max (later Matt), has had the treatment. He moves to the South in pursuit of a white woman who snubbed him (when he was

Black) in a Harlem night club. While there, he becomes the leader of one of the most racists groups in the country, the Knights of Nordica. He uses their treasury to make himself a multimillionaire. Then he thwarts their efforts to kill any number of black people.

He finds the girl, who falls madly in love *with his money*, at first. Problems arise when there are no more black people to do the menial, but essential jobs in the country.

Can America exist with only one race? Schuyler's answer to that question is hilarious, but troubling.

Humor also features prominently in Rudolph Fisher's murder mystery, *The Conjure-Man Dies*.

Fisher's protagonist is Dr. John Archer, "A tall, slender, light-skinned man of obviously habitual composure…. who practices in Harlem."

Dr. Archer is called to address an urgent case across the street from his brownstone. Sadly, the would-be patient, one of the doctor's neighbors, is beyond any help the physician can give.

The gentleman who brings Dr. Archer to the scene of the crime is quite a character.

"And you—if I don't presume?"

"Me? I'm Bubber Brown—"

"Well, how did this happen, Mr. Brown?"

" 'Deed I don't know, doc. What you mean—is somebody killed him?"

Bubber and his sidekick Jinx are a combination of Amos and Andy and King Lear's fool.

The victim was a psychic named Frimbo, with a gift for fortune telling and a small fortune. He lived in a Harlem that

Fisher makes clear is a world unto itself of *de facto* segregation. Consequently, the New York Police Department sends an all-black police unit to the crime scene. The detective assigned to the case is a man named Perry Dart:

"Of the ten Negro members of Harlem's police force to be promoted from the rank of patrolman to that of detective, Perry Dart was one of the first."

However, while describing Perry and indeed all of the novel's characters, Fisher appears to be color struck.

"As if the city administration had wished to leave no doubt in the public mind as to its intention in the matter, they had chosen in him a man who could not have been under any circumstances mistaken for aught but a Negro; or perhaps, as Dart's intimates insisted, they had chosen him because his generously pigmented skin rendered him invisible in the dark, a conceivably great advantage to a detective who did most of his work at night." Then Fisher explains that Dart's dark skin doesn't impair his intelligence.

Dart directs the murder investigation and recruits Dr. Archer to assist him. The pair quickly learns that the victim was very reclusive, but he had powerful enemies. Among them was the numbers runner Spider Webb, who under Dart's interrogation, outlines his problem with the murdered man:

"This Frimbo was a smart guy—much too smart," Spider Webb began.

"Yes?"

"Yea. He had a system of playing the game that couldn't lose. I don't know how he did it—whether he worked out somethin' mathematical or was just a good guesser or what. But he could hit regular once a week without fail."

In short, the crime boss couldn't afford to pay out so much. Frimbo, according to Webb, could either stop winning or stop living. Frimbo does die--for a time. Then he comes back to life and explains to the police that he can rise from the dead. Now they must decide if they should investigate a murder that no longer has a murder victim. In the meantime, Webb is just one of a growing number of suspects in this maybe murder.

Death comes stalking unequivocally in Langston Hughes' only novel, *Not Without Laughter*. Unlike the other three novels in this volume, there is very little humor in this book. Hughes is writing about the death of the soul and the death of soul mates.

In this coming of age, autobiographical novel, Sandy, a young Black boy, is being raised primarily by his grandmother, Aunt Hager. It is pre-WWI Kansas. We meet the two as they barely escape a cyclone. They prepare to go to the home of their white neighbor because she has a cellar in which they can ride out the storm safely.

"It's a cyclone! It's gwine be a cyclone! Sandy, let's get over to Mis' Carter's quick,'cause we ain't got no cellar here. Con on, chile, let's get! Come on, chile!...Come on, chile!"....

"Aunt Hagar opened the front door, but before she or the child could move, a great roaring sound suddenly shook the world, and, with a deafening division of wood from wood, they saw their front porch rise into the air and go hurtling off into space."

The two huddled inside their small cabin. The twister is in some ways a metaphor for the boy's life. An only child, he is the center of his grandmother's and mother Anjee's world. Sandy's two aunts dote on him also, but differently.

Hughes characterizes the youngest Aunt Harriett as a free spirit. There is little opportunity for a black woman in the

South who has little education and who doesn't want to be a maid or a laundress.

"What for?" Harriett retorted angrily. "There's plenty what for! All that work for five dollars a week with what little tips those pikers give you. And white men insulting you besides, asking you to sleep with 'em. Look at my finger-nails, all broke from scrubbing that dining-room floor."

His Aunt Tempy is cold and withdrawn. She has married well, and avoids her poverty stricken family. When Aunt Hager dies, Tempy takes Sandy in. Still, Tempy is a loveless woman and no ally to the boy.

Unlike the other three novels in this volume, Hughes' work addresses the issue of the poor working class. This is the generation after slavery. These are the descendants of slaves whose parents and grandparents left the South for a better life in the Midwest. What they found was a variation on the same theme: segregation and menial jobs.

For Black men, finding work was excruciatingly hard. Jimboy, Sandy's father, was seldom at home because he was always looking for work:

"Jimboy was always going, but Aunt Hager was wrong about his never working. It was just that he couldn't stay in one place all the time. ...Besides, what was there in Stanton anyhow for a young colored fellow to do except dig sewer ditches for a few cents an hour or maybe porter around a store for seven dollars a week."

Not Without Laughter is a meditative work that gently depicts some harsh realities of Black American life. Yet it ends on a hopeful note. Sandy is on his way to an education that will change his life.

Each of the novels in this volume is a legacy. All of the authors are gifted.

They bring craft and insight to record the heroic struggles of black people in combating racism and its antecedents, segregation and slavery.

Editor Rafia Zafar deserves thanks and praise for her decision first to republish these novels, and second, to include "authoritative texts and a chronology, biographies, and notes reflecting the latest scholarship" in these works. She also included passages that had been edited out of several of the novels when they were first published. These volumes are a gift to our community and the literary community as a whole, and so is she.

The Harlem Renaissance Revisited: Politics, Arts, and Letters

by Jeffrey O.G. Ogbar (Editor)

Johns Hopkins University Press | 2010

Reviewed by Sarah Vogelsong

Jeffery O. G. Ogbar

The Harlem Renaissance has always been an appealing moment in American history, but never more so than in times of economic hardship, when little distraction from uncertainty and dull necessity seem to exist. In a period of contraction and austerity, any flowering of culture serves as a powerful reaffirmation of a society's value and provides something to counteract the apparent meaninglessness of the daily struggle.

In light of the current recession, Jeffrey O. G. Ogbar's recent collection of scholarship, *The Harlem Renaissance Revisited: Politics, Arts, and Letters*, is well timed. One essay in particular, *Back to Harlem: Abstract and Everyday Labor during the Harlem Renaissance*, by Jacob S. Dorman, strikes a chord in the attention it devotes to "the masses of people who lined [Harlem's] streets"—the majority of whom faced backbreaking labor and wearying unemployment alternately, as well as a prohibitively high cost of living (Dorman observes that many Harlem residents, especially families with children, were forced to take in boarders) and consistent discrimination. Dorman rightly notes that "the abstracted Harlem of the literary imagination" has overshadowed the reality of life for most of the neighborhood's inhabitants in the public mind.

Despite this insightful chapter and the concluding essay of the collection that focuses on the fascinating phenomenon of

African American travel and involvement in Soviet Russia from the 1920s up to the beginning of World War II (Maxim Matusevich's *Harlem Globetrotters: Black Sojourners in Stalin's Soviet Union*), most of Ogbar's articles focus on the art and literature produced in Harlem during this era. It is possibly because these subjects have been treated so thoroughly within the canon that this focus seems detrimental to the book as a whole.

What new insight is Ogbar able to unearth in this volume—what in these pages makes Harlem worth "revisiting"? There are certainly a number of reasons for such a trip, but Ogbar seems to have not been able to choose one—and so, jamming them all between two covers, the final product lacks focus.

The volume thus raises two important questions: First, why does Ogbar's collection seem so little concerned with what aspects of the Harlem Renaissance we can bring to bear upon American society at the beginning of the twenty-first century? Second, what are these aspects?

Regarding the first question: Literature and arts scholarship can all too easily fall into the trap of insularity. In the humanities disciplines, scholars pride themselves on a certain purity of approach that examines the works in question under a microscope, as if they existed in a vacuum. Even those studies that do take into account societal currents and the flaws and desires of the work's creator—seeing the work as both a product of the times and as something to be interacted with and that affects change in the world at that moment—still fail to extend this consideration to the present time. How does the work affect and interact with us today? Why and how does it continue to have meaning for us? These problems aren't helped by the need of our academics to secure tenure; for many, the solution on which they fix is to study, in exhaustive detail, minor works that have been ignored—often with reason. Ogbar's collection seems to fall into this trap.

The second question is probably more important and more open to interpretation. Last autumn, I had the privilege of attending a lecture at the City University of New York on the Depression that addressed the question of how an economic crisis impacts the arts. The panel of speakers offered three examples: a crisis exacerbates critique of the present circumstances; the arts receive new sources of support; and a crisis leads to the construction of a new kind of audience and public. Art becomes more accessible during a crisis, because people start to understand the vital necessity of the arts and literature to their lives.

Although the Harlem Renaissance predated the Depression, the economic reality faced by black Americans in the earlier era was similar to the later period faced by the nation as a whole. The art that was produced during the

Harlem Renaissance was created in the face of great hardship and yet it was able to break new ground in modes of communication, in intensity of critique, and in the transformation of its audience.

We live in an era when marginalized groups are increasingly raising their voices, but we have not yet seen the same kind of artistic outpouring that the Harlem Renaissance saw. It would have been interesting had Ogbar's collection consistently investigated not only the inner workings of the literature, but also the kind of response that they received. Essays such as *So the Girl Marries*, concerning the DuBois-Cullen marriage, touch on both points and are able to provide insight into the perspectives of people at the time (and how similar many of their reactions seem to those expressed today!). But others are sorely lacking in this department and risk pushing the Harlem

Renaissance onto the back burner of a dusty academic shelf, which would certainly be a loss to us all.

The City of Light and the Making of American Writers

An essay by Fred Beauford

For reasons I cannot fully understand, for the last few years I have become obsessed with reading biographies of 20th Century American writers; madly almost, until book after book finally led me to those writers who came to the conclusion that exile from America was the only way they could ever fully realize their talents as creative writers in a uncharted post war world, first with Ernest Hemingway's "Lost Generation" and their long, slow journey by sea to the fable City of Light.

Hemingway's shell-shocked generation was still walking in the bloody footsteps of the most horrendous shedding of human blood by other humans in recorded history; what we call World War One.

It was also clear that The Lost Generation was seeking small, fun filled caves with like-minded souls, to slowly lick their wounds and seek something meaningful other than material things and more warfare.

American writers first discovered Paris as *the* place to be for artists because of a newspaperman and political activist from New England named Henry Clapp, Jr. In August 1849, Clapp went to Paris to attend a three-day world peace congress, where he found a city that had just experienced a revolution the year before he arrived, and "the boulevards of Paris still thrummed with idealism, slogans and grand artistic schemes. The city's cafes played host to a thriving scene, known as Bohemianism," writes Justin Martin in *Rebel Souls: Walt Whitman and America's First Bohemians*

After the experience of Paris, and the vibrant artistic atmosphere-- made even more so by the instant sensation on November 22, 1849 of the play *La Vie de Boheme,* which Puccini later adapted in 1896 for his classic opera, *La Boheme*—there was no way that Clapp could return to New England. Instead, he moved to New York City, determined to bring to America the Bohemia he had experience in Paris. And bring it he did, and he single-handedly started the mystique of The City of Light in America.

***

It was Gertrude Stein—Paris's abiding spirit and prominent literary hostess—who coined the phrase "The Lost Generation" in conversation with Ernest Hemingway.

"You are all a lost generation," she said to him.

These "lost" American writers that often cross path with Stein and Hemingway, included folks like, Hart Crane, Ezra Pound and F. Scott Fitzgerald and his wife, the notorious Zelda Fitzgerald of legend.

Notwithstanding the highly entertaining drunken antics of the Fitzgerald's, my personal favorites among this crowd of lost souls from America, have always been Sara Murphy, and her husband, the some times painter Gerald Murphy.

Although marginally literary, the pair was great to look at, both being exceptional good looking; and they were also very rich, fashionable, loved writers, and was well known for the famous line, "Living well is the best revenge "

During this period these American exiles encountered not only the famous Murphys, but interacted with *"any number of intersecting artistic cliques including Modernists and Cubists, Dadaists and Futurists, Expressionists and Surrealists. These were the years of Picasso and Modigliani, Braque and Duchamp, Stravinski and Satie, Diaghilev and Cocteau. Radical developments in the visual and performing arts were mirrored in the Continental literature of the time, from the surrealist shock tactics of André Bréton and Guillaume Apollinaire, to the textual experimentation of Joyce and Beckett. It was into this vibrant, inspiring foment of idea and innovation that the self-imposed exiles of America's "Lost Generation" flung themselves."*

(Editor's note: this highly dramatic quote is from a book entitled *The Lost Generation*, but as I tried to find the exact book it was taken from, and posted online, I found over 500 titles of the same name. Obviously, The Lost Generation has had its fair share of admirers).

***

And, after another horrifying world war in as little as over twenty years later, we find American writers once again trying to make sense of a world that seems to go mad every twenty years, almost on cue.

During most of the late 40s and early 50s, American intellectuals and artists, as shell-shocked as the Lost Generation, having witness slaughter beyond belief, ended up once again in the same place as The Lost Generation: the fable City of Light, Paris.

Now we have yet another great wave of American artists' infatuated with Paris. Even black American writers like Richard Wright, James Baldwin, the often overlooked Chester Hines, the then dancer, poet/memoirist Maya Angelo, all fled to Paris, where they encountered Simone Lucie Ernestine Marie Bertrand de Beauvoir, Edith Piaf, Sartre, a much older Picasso, Camus, and countless white

American writers like James Jones, Norman Mailer, Christopher Isherwood, Saul Bellow, Philip Roth and Truman Capote, all doing the "Paris bohemian thing," as Baldwin might say.

And as much as these brilliant writers felt that they had to fled an uptight, militaristic, anti-gay, anti-interracial couples, racist America, most soon realized that they were Americans after all, that there was indeed something called an American.

When they looked at each closely, they saw a part of themselves, especially when they discovered how marginalized the Arabs were in France. Black and white, gay or not, well off, or barely getting by, they immediately recognized what that was all about. They had grown up with these kinds of characters, and came to the City of Light in the first place, to get away from them. But there they now were.

And, like the Lost Generation before them, these writers also had an even stronger pull back to America. France was still suffering from the last war, and was trying to hold on to what was left of its once mighty colonial power, especially Algeria.

America was never a real colonial player, like Britain and France, and after both world wars, it quickly went back to what it did best: make a lot of people rich. This country was still the most dynamic country on earth, and there were grants, awards, and magazines to write for; book companies were pining away for their services. And there was new thing called television, which could give them more fame than they ever hoped for.

And once again, what really made America exciting for these creative writers, like those ex-pats before then, was this was where the action was, where clouds of turmoil were slowly gathering, where it looked as if old wounds could at last be addressed.

What else could such a writer want? This was the New World.

Richard Wright and Chester Himes, with Himes finally settling in Franco's Spain, refused to leave Europe. Henry Miller stayed longer then most, and James Baldwin never fully gave up on France, and spent most of his adult life going back and forth between the two counties, with many stops in Istanbul. He died at the age of 63, December 1, 1987 at Saint-Paul de Vence in the South of France.

Those that left for good did not give up bohemia, however, when they decided to return home, and stayed true to their bohemian roots, started by Henry Clapp, and soon settled in North Beach in San Francisco, and Greenwich Village in New York City, which had become mother's milk for creative writers and essayists, despite the heady hedonism of wine, women (and hot young boys) and American jazz, of Paris.

"Yes, I am an American," most ultimately said, including a deeply conflicted, wavering Baldwin, who despite his saying he was just a novelist, and leave him alone to do his art, he became the spokesman and conscious of the Civil Rights Generation in America, and like the others, sailed back home more than eager to join in the debate that was now unfolding in their country.

Lloyd Richards:

Teacher, Director, Friend

BY WOODIE KING, JR.

When Lloyd Richard died in New York City, June 29, 2006 on his 87th birthday, the American theatre lost one of the most influential Black theatre artists of the last century. Lloyd's enlightenment caught fire in Detroit.

Detroit is where I began my theatrical career. When I graduated Cass Tech High School in 1956, all I knew about theatre was that the same white faces I had seen in the movies peopled it. I loved the movies. In 1958, with no history of theatre anywhere in my family, a movie titled The Defiant Ones, starring Sidney Poitier changed my life forever: A black man saying and doing things I had never seen on screen before! ! Who was Sidney Poi tier? Thus, the journey of who and how did he arrive at that place: to be starring in a major motion picture?

The Detroit Public Library and librarian, Kirk Meyers, led me into the world of Sidney Poi tier and The American Negro Theatre (you, the Reader, must examine Sidney Poitier's history). But first, what about theater right here in Detroit? What about David Rambeau, Cliff Frazier, Walter Mason, Gil Maddox, Alma Forest Parks (who worked with Sidney at the American Negro Theatre), Powell Lindsey, Maggie Porter?

David Rambeau taught me the importance of knowledge; Dave loved black art and black theatre. I sought out Ron Milner; Walter Mason, through his impressionable work as an actor and sophistication, led me to Lloyd Richards. Lloyd Richards brought me back again to Sidney Poitier. Sidney and Lloyd studied acting together with Paul Mann in New York (so .. .1 must study acting ...)

So, I enrolled in Wayne University to study acting. At Wayne University Lloyd Richards was a hero. And then, in 1958, late in the year, *A Raisin in the Sun*, directed by the hero, and starring his friend Sidney Poitier, changed the way American's viewed Black theatre.

Two years after A Raisin in the Sun closed Lloyd started teaching Acting again. I arrived in New York City in March 1964. Walter Mason led me directly to Lloyd Richards. I was immediately accepted in Lloyd's Professional Acting Studio. The studio was located on West 29th Street. Classmates I remember Lloyd working into fine actors were J.B. Abercrombie, Connie Booth, Judith Byrd, Leu Camacho, Lucretia Collins, Cecilia Cooper, Nate Caldwell, Herb Davis, Rick Ferrell, Merv Haines, Mel Hopson, Tina Sattin, Pawnee Sills, Gabrille Strassun, Charles Turner, and Selena Williams.

Lloyd's teaching method was brilliant and yet very basic: he very carefully phrased questions and sought clarity from each of us about our intent in a scene. Through his take on Stanislavski, he led us directly to the character and the through line of the action.

Lloyd let me take care of his studio. I was euphoric! I mopped the floor, took messages, kept attendance, collected fees, and put the chairs in order. I remember answering the telephone when he got the call from Lore Noto to direct The Yearling; from Joseph Kipness to direct I Had A Ball; and the Oneill Theatre Center. Students from the class - including Charles Turner - accompanied Lloyd and Walter Mason to Waterford, Connecticut to build the theater center for its first play, Joel Oliansky's Bedford Forest. I studied Acting with Lloyd until May 1967. In 1966 I asked Lloyd to direct my friend Ron Milner's Who's Got His Own. He accepted. Glynn

Turman (who had played Travis in Lloyd's production of A Raisin in the Sun), played the lead.

In a world of artists who are only capable of paving the road once the jungle has been cleared and a pathway exists, Lloyd had no such pathway for his work with Loraine Hansberry and August Wilson. It was Lloyd and Lloyd all alone who placed Black theater's new voices in the mainstream of American Theatre. He directed six of Wilson's ten plays on Broadway; Ma Rainey's Black Bottom (1984); Fences (1987), for which Lloyd received the Tony Award; Joe Turner's Come and Gone (1988); The Piano Lesson (1990); Two Trains Running (1992); and Seven Guitars (1996).

In his busy breakneck years as Director of Yale School of Drama, and Yale Repertory Theater, and the O'Neill Playwrights Conference (1979 through the mid 90's) we made dozens of trips to both institutions.

Lloyd was driven by righteousness. Listen to Lloyd in a conversation with me in March 2002 for TDF Sightlines: "

when we opened in Philadelphia with *A Raisin in the Sun,* the audience was about 90% white. In three days the audience was over 50% black, and that's where the story came in. I was standing in the lobby of the theatre looking at the people lined up to buy tickets. There was a woman who was at the ticket window who gave the treasurer one dollar. The treasurer told her the ticket is $4.80. She exclaimed, '$4.80?1 I can see Sidney Poitier around the corner in a movie for ninety-five cents.' She went into that pocketbook and got out the rest of her money and bought a ticket and started walking into the theater. It was only 3pm, so the treasurer tells her that she couldn't go in now, she'd have to come back at 8:30. I stopped her and asked her why she was paying $4.80 to see Sidney when she could pay ninety-five cents around the corner. She said 'The word's out in my neighborhood that something's going on down here that concerns me, so I had to come down and find out what it was all about.' At that moment I knew why I was in the theatre, and what I was doing there. "

Lloyd did stay the course. He had an awesome dedication. And commitment. An example: For five days, June 18-23, 2002, he forced himself - while in a wheelchair -to attend a playwrights' conference in Valdez, Alaska. While there, he gave advice and conducted workshops for young playwrights. In his last years he became obsessed with leaving all the information he had amassed over his long career in the hands of generations to follow. In addition to his teaching at The Actor's Center (New York), he commuted to Bennington College; recorded a history of his journey, which was taped November 16, 2004, for the Theater on Film and Tape Archives for New York Public Library; and in the soon to be released documentary, Segregating the Greatest

Generation, Lloyd speaks eloquently on how World War II impacted his life and his relationship to white America. Segregating had its world-premiere February 4, 2007.

Lloyd only directed me once: In 1967. But as teacher, director, and friend, Lloyd and I shared a 42-year association. My last meeting with Lloyd was at his home in April 2006. He was meeting and giving advice to Dr. Von Washington; though not in good health, Lloyd graciously granted Von two hours.

I would like to thank his wife Barbara for sharing her husband with the American Theatre; and a special thank you to his sons Scott and Thomas. •

Literary Brooklyn: The Writers of Brooklyn and the Story of American City Life

by Evan Hughes

Reviewed by Fred Beauford

Credit: Amy Wilton

On the Waterfront

I have a confession to make that might just shock some of you old time readers of this magazine, given my ongoing, shameless display of Bronx chauvinism, and my obvious distaste and love of bashing Brooklyn every chance I get.

In the army, as a teenage wise guy from New York City, I strutted about like a young peacock, grabbing my crouch at every chance, and talked much trash and acted like the know-it-all I still am.

I told all the guys I was from Brooklyn, trying my best to talk out of the side of my mouth, as they looked on at me in slightly baffled amusement.

For some reason, Brooklyn just sounded more badass than being from the unsung Bronx, with only the white shoe Yankees to brag about.

There, it's finally off my chest, and I feel better already.

***

Brooklyn outclassed us rubes in the Bronx in terms of literary output as well, not being satisfied with being the widely acknowledged tough guys of New York City. In fact, Evan Hughes' highly entertaining literary history lesson, *Literary Brooklyn: The Writers of Brooklyn and the Story of American City Life,* shows us that Brooklyn also gave Manhattan's famed Greenwich Village a run for its money as a haven for creative writers.

We touched on this once in the *Neworld Review,* in Jan Alexander's groundbreaking essay on Carson McCullers, and her stay at 7 Middagh Street in Brooklyn Heights, made famous in the book, *February House* by Sherill Tippins, which she shared with, among others, W.H. Auden, Klaus Mann and Gypsy Rose Lee.

Hughes gives us engaging portraits of off and on Brooklyn literary residents like Walt Whitman, Henry Miller, Hart Crane, Marianne Moore, Thomas Wolfe, Richard Wright, the aforementioned *February House*, Truman Cupote, William Styron and Norman Mailer, among others.

His concise, well-researched biographic sketches of the writers in *Literary Brooklyn* are fully brought to life, and are alone well worth the price of the book.

***

Because this is also a book about the physical and economic development of Brooklyn, Hughes provides the proper context for why it became such a magnet for literary types.

When Walt Whitman, “the grandfather of literary Brooklyn,” first arrived as a child of three, in 1823, “it was a place so different from the huge urban mass of today…that it is scarcely possible to hold it in the mind’s eye,” Hughes writes.

One interesting historical tidbit around this time jumped out at me from his book: “In 1800, before slaveholding was abolished in New York State, in 1827, about 60 percent of the white households within Brooklyn's current borders owned at least one slave, the highest proportion in the north," he writes.

In the first years of his 30s, Whitman was writing his self-published masterpiece, *Leaves of Grass*, which Hughes points out, "drew breath from the people of Brooklyn." A little over ten years later, at the eve of the Civil War, Brooklyn had grown from a quiet little village of five thousand during Whitman's childhood, to the nation's third largest city.

"Part of what spurred the growth," Hughes writes, "was Brooklyn's investment in an industrial waterfront that competed with Manhattan's. By the time that Henry Miller's family moved to Williamsburg in the early 1890s soon after his birth, this is what Manhattan had become, as *Harper's* magazine had noted a few decades earlier: 'What was then a decent and orderly town of moderate size, has been converted into a huge semi-barbarous metropolis—one half as luxurious and artistic as Paris, the other half as savage as Cairo and Constantinople—not well-governed, but simply not governed at all'."

Hughes points out that "by the time Miller was born, Brooklyn had become something of a release valve, a place New Yorkers came in search of a haven, but also a place where trouble tended to follow them."

And come they did. In fact, so many Jews fled the crowded tenements of lower Manhattan that soon over 40 percent of Jews in New York were living in Brooklyn. By this time, Brooklyn was no longer a separate city, but had joined with the rest of New York, much to the dismay of many of its citizens.

Manhattan was becoming a polarized place of lavish townhouses and mansions for the well-off, and dismal tenements for almost everyone else, which eventually led to the building of the famous brownstones that Brooklyn is still famous for, as well as attached houses and roomy apartment buildings, all kept to a smaller scale than Manhattan or the Bronx.

People got to know each other in Brooklyn neighborhoods, which only added to the borough's charm and rapid growth.

But a seamier side of Brooklyn had also begun to emerge, especially around the docks where most of the creative writers ended up because of the cheap rent (I can still hear Marlon Brando overacting in *On the Waterfront:* "I could have been a contender, instead of a bum.").

Longshoremen and sailors from all over the world, the marginal, the sex- obsessed and lowlifes of all kinds, ages, shapes, and colors, all crowded the many bars and dives that dotted the landscape.

Unlike the sedate poet Marianne Moore, who lived quietly further inland, in Fort Green with her mother, novelists like Henry Miller and Thomas Wolfe relished the constant two-fisted challenge to self from the docks, and drew much from the dangerous, volatile world of the waterfront.

For gay poets like W. H, Auden and Hart Crane, who often came back to their housing battered and bruised, they had the thrilling adventure of cruising Sands Street, with its many "sailor bars," seeking that perfect sailor—the one that would most captured their imaginations, and provide the muse they long sought.

***

In time, due to the earlier influx of Jews, as noted, Brooklyn, starting with the depression years of the 30s, started producing an amazing group of Jewish writers. For most of these writers, it wasn't a tough guy persona, or even writing the great American novel, filled with the hapless riffraff of Sands Street, they wanted most to write about.

What they wanted to project to the world was raw intelligence, the value of education, knowing things, and deep insights into the human condition. In other words, there was nothing wrong with being an intellectual.

Evan Hughes once again is highly impressive with his portraits of Daniel Fuchs, Bernard Malamud, and Alfred Kazin, among others.

***

Another American mass movement of people also took place, which would soon have a tremendous impact on Brooklyn: the great migration of millions of blacks fleeing the fascist south. Here is where Richard Wright takes center stage in *Literary Brooklyn.*

Richard Wright is more than just a footnote in American literary history. He was one of the first that held up the unblinking mirror to America, both black and white, that said, this is who you really are.

He wrote his two most famous books, *Native Son*, and *Black Boy* in Brooklyn.

***

Literary Brooklyn skillfully brings us up to present day Brooklyn, after taking the reader through the great collapse of the wartime economy, including another interesting historical tidbit: The Brooklyn Navy Yard produced more ships during World War Two than all of Japan!

We start to see rapid urban decline and despair, reflected best by Hubert Selby, Jr.'s grim, in your face *Last Exit to Brooklyn,* and Arthur Miller's tale of economic defeat in *Death of a Salesman*, which had Brooklyn written all over it, but which struck an accord with all of America, most of whom were enduring some of the same change of events, often with the same dismal results that the confused, deeply disappointed Willy Loman faced.

***

In the end, Brooklyn was slowly brought back to life, first by the pioneering "brownstoners," who bought sturdy, but well-worn dwellings (a special nod should go to those many African American women who have helped maintain this historical housing), when no one with any good sense wanted to come anywhere near certain areas of Brooklyn. Then the artists started coming, led by people like filmmaker Spike Lee, and the Village Voice writer Nelson George.

Suddenly, Brooklyn was cool again.

Again, like in years past, it offered the affordable rent that one could not find in Manhattan, as even the once trashy

East Village was now overrun with big pocketed, Wall Street types.

Hughes gives us a passing look at present day Brooklyn creative writers including Jhumpa Lahiri, Colson Whitehead, Jennifer Egan, Rick Moody, Jonathan Safran Foer, Susan Choi, Nathan Englander, Nicole Krauss, Darin Strauss, Kurt Andersen, Arthur Phillips, Julie Orringer, Rivka Galchen, Keith Gessen, Hannah Tinti, Tim McLoughlin and Jonathan Ames.

***

Literary Brooklyn: The Writers of Brooklyn and the Story of American City Life is a wonderful literary history lesson, well told, and I was sad that it had to end. I once again thank my friends at Henry Holt for sending me yet another compelling book to review, and thank author Evan Hughes for writing it;

and if he would ever like to write for the *Neworld Review,* he is more than welcome.

It's books like *Literary Brooklyn* that cause you to not only walk the streets of Brooklyn, but also Manhattan, my beloved Bronx, Queens, and even lowly Staten Island, all of which have played huge roles in America's literary history--and hear countless stories, some beyond awful, some beyond wonderful, some beyond belief--and makes one feel proud to have grown up in New York, and to have reached one of the highest honors this great city bestows, that of a literary editor and publisher.

By Loretta H. Campbell

Hazel Scott: The Pioneering Journey of a Jazz Pianist from Café Society to Hollywood to HUAC

By Karen Chilton

The University of Michigan Press: Ann Arbor. Ann Arbor, Michigan 2008, ISBN-13:978-0-472-11567-9 ISBN-10:0-472-11567-7 $29.95

p. 83. "Until my fight at Columbia, no Black person had even dared oppose the Establishment. You either kept your mouth shut and took the roles you could get or you remained out of work." —Hazel Scott

Always in the vanguard, Hazel Scott never lowered her professional standards or lost her nerve, as author Karen Chilton, (co-author of *I Wish you Love: A Memoir of Gloria Lynn*) illustrates in this measured biography. During the segregated abyss of 1943, Scott defied Harry Cohn, the head of Hollywood's Columbia Pictures.

Cohn's nickname was King Cohn because he ruled the studio and brooked no questions about his orders. He and Scott had a head-to-head confrontation during the filming of the movie, *The Heat's On* in which Scott had a small but significant role. In one scene of the film, the sweethearts and wives of Black soldiers are seeing their men off to war. Cohn okayed a decision to have these women wearing dirty dresses with messy hair. Scott insisted that Black women would dress in their best to see their loved ones off to war. When the director wouldn't change the scene, she went on a three-day strike effectively stopping the production. Cohn agreed to her demands, but told her she would never work in Hollywood again as long as he lived. He made good on that promise. Her movie career in the U.S. languished for 20 years.

Fortunately, Scott remained one of the highest paid jazz pianists in the world aptly named the "darling of café society, as Chilton outlines." This was because Scott, a child prodigy, had been "woodshedding her work from the age of three. At that age, she created her first piano, of sorts. She played the floor of the family's parlor in their native Trinidad. When her grandmother saw her, she put Scott on the real piano. She played it so well that her grandmother called the neighbors to watch. Not only had Scott never had a lesson, she had never played the piano before. She learned the keys by watching her mother, Alma, teach piano.

Alma's own dreams of being a concert pianist were thwarted because of her weak wrists. She became her daughter's first teacher and imposed strict practice rules on Scott. As a result, Scott's technique and skill were strong. However, while her skills were getting her little gigs around their community, Alma's work was drying up. Ever resourceful, Alma moved her small family to Harlem, NY. (Scott's father had abandoned the family many years before. He occasionally resurfaced, but they had no real relationship). Once there, Alma took up various enterprises to support them.

When these businesses didn't work, she went back to what she knew—music. Scott recalled, "Months of contemplation led her to a choice that was as unlikely as it was unexpected. The saxophone. She would learn to play the saxophone. Without further consideration and very little discussion, she went down to a local music shop, rented a tenor sax, and sat down to teach herself the instrument. " ' My mother started to learn the saxophone and she would practice in our tiny living room.'"

Alma became so proficient that she supported her family by playing for and with some of the great musicians of her day. Among them Lil Hardin, Valaida Snow, Duke

Ellington, Billie Holiday, and the priceless Mary Lou Williams. Because of her mother's talent and connections, Scott grew up with these extraordinary musicians as mentors and friends. When she was ready to step out on her own, they were part of her large extended family.

Chilton's describes Scott's support system as not only artists in jazz. It included classical pianists and teachers. As a result of these and her prodigious talent, she was given an audition at New York's Julliard School—at the age of eight. The requisite age for an audition was 16. However, Alma had somehow convinced the school administrators to hear her daughter. Scott so impressed them, including the head of Julliard, Dr. Frank Damrosch and Professor Oscar Wagner that they admitted Hazel and gave her private lessons.

By the time she was fifteen, Scott was the featured attraction in nightclubs and working with the brightest lights of American classical music. She created a hybrid of boogie woogie and European classical music that garnered her fans around the world. She grew up in the music so to speak.

While still in her twenties, she commanded high salaries in clubs and in movies. She made recordings for several labels. Chilton has provided a scholarly list of Scott's discography and a list of her movie and television roles in the back of the book.

Scott also met and fell in love with Adam Clayton Powell, Jr. Chilton describes the marriage as troubled from the beginning. The fact that the Powells were both celebrities made their private lives public. However, Chilton lets her research speak for itself. The facts are never colored with tabloidism.

Powell was 11 years Scott's senior and married to the actress Isabel Washington when he wooed Hazel. The

Scott/Powell affair resulted in his divorce. Shortly, afterward, the two of them married. Initially, Scott's income was nearly twice that of Powell's. The couple lived lavishly. She had her own dress maker, hair dresser, and jeweler. However, Powell persuaded her to limit her career choices in order to have more time for their marriage. The union lasted eleven years, and the couple have a son, Adam Clayton Powell, III.

During their marriage, they weathered many storms from without and within. The most famous of these was the House on UnAmerican Activities (HUAC). Because many of Scott's friends were avowed communists, and she herself was outspoken on Civil Rights issues, she was targeted as a communist. She wasn't. Nonetheless, she found that HUAC had labeled her as such. The fact that she was the wife of now Senator Adam Clayton Powell, Jr. made no difference, Chilton emphasizes.

Once again defying convention, Scott asked to speak before HUAC before being subpoenaed. She was granted a meeting, but it was too late. She was effectively blacklisted, Chilton explains. Scott went aboard to Europe for work. Her marriage to Powell was faltering because of his numerous extramarital affairs. It finally collapsed, and the couple divorced. Scott raised their son, nicknamed Skipper, alone.

Scott remarried briefly to a white Italian named Ezio Bedin. They too divorced amicably. However, earning a living in Europe became difficult for Scott despite the fact that she spoke seven languages. Work dried up, and her career all but died. When she returned to America over a decade later, her career and she had lost most of the celebrity she had enjoyed.

Chilton describes the last years of Scott's life as delicately as she had Scott's halcyon days. Scott got her dream job and called her son to proclaim the happy news.

"I've got great news. This is fantastic news. Your mother has her dream job. Joe Kipnus says he's going to open a new room on 45th Street and he wants to name it after me. I can play as many weeks a year as I want.... 'Well, you know the superstition. When you get your dream job, you're going to die.' "

Scott played in the club for a week or two. A few weeks later, Hazel Scott died of pancreatic cancer.

Pops: A Life of Louis Armstrong

By Terry Teachout

496 pages | Houghton Mifflin Harcourt

Reviewed by Ken Liebeskind

New biography doesn't spare criticism of America's foremost trumpeter

Louis Armstrong was "a black man born at the turn of the century in the poorest quarter of New Orleans, who, by the end of his life, was known and loved in every corner of the earth," Terry Teachout writes near the beginning of Pops, the new biography of Armstrong that doesn't completely tarnish the notion of the well loved Armstrong, but challenges it with lucid depictions of the criticism that was directed at his music and personality, coming from all sides.

Blacks and whites were highly critical of his music, which regressed from the vigorous Dixieland jazz of his early days, to the schmaltzy pop of his later years. Straight ahead jazz musicians like Dizzy Gillespie and Miles Davis condemned Armstrong, as did white jazz critics and mainstream publications, from Time magazine to The New York Times.

There are a number of reasons Armstrong's music faltered – from his inability to adapt his popular style to the new streams in jazz, which left traditionalists like Armstrong aside - to the fact that he was managed by a man who did whatever he could to milk Armstrong for the money he could bring in by playing popular music.

Teachout writes that Armstrong had nothing but contempt for bebop, while the beboppers thought him ancient. Of course when bebop took fire in the early 1950's, Armstrong's career was already 30 years old. But instead of jamming with the avant-garde musicians, he continued recording pop songs, first with big bands and later with his small band of All Stars. To Armstrong, bebop was "threatening to the public's acceptance of jazz," Teachout writes. He preferred to "offer his listeners music they could enjoy without exertion."

Another reason Armstrong's music is criticized is because he spent so much time singing, which transformed him from a jazz trumpeter to a popular entertainer. While he was initially a compelling scat singer, replacing the words to "'Heebie Jeebies' with improvised nonsense syllables," in a 1926 recording that was highly renowned, he went on to become a sappy pop singer. His biggest hit was "Hello Dolly," the number one best seller he claims to have performed "six jillion" times that was condemned by the music critic Gunther Schuller as an example of Armstrong singing "against a cheap Dixieland sextet (over a soggy string section yet)."

Armstrong's move to record and perform popular music reflects his desire to "sing prettier for the white people whose favor he sought to curry," Teachout writes. The same can be said for his performances in popular films, including Pennies from Heaven and Cabin in the Sky, which embarrassed blacks and white critics who called him a "picturesque, Sambo style entertainer."

Dizzy Gillespie called him a "plantation character" in a Downbeat interview, and Armstrong himself admitted that "some of my own people have accused me of being an Uncle Tom, of not being aggressive."

Armstrong couldn't take strong racial stands because it would have threatened his career. He was forced to perform before racially exclusive audiences in the South through much of his career; and he relied on whites to manage his career, white record companies to record him and white club owners to allow him to perform. Teachout says Armstrong took the advice of Benny Williams, a fellow black from New Orleans, who told him to "always have a white man (who like you) and can and will put his hand on your shoulder and say – "This is 'My' Nigger and, Can't Nobody Harm Ya."

The white man who played that role for Armstrong was his long time manager, Joe Glaser, the underworld figure who Armstrong deferred to without complaint. Teachout says he was subservient.

Armstrong frequently performed with white musicians and there are compelling portraits of his relations with Barney Bigard, the clarinetist, and Jack Teagarden, the trombonist, who was perhaps Armstrong's favorite all-time accompanist. "More than a friend, Teagarden was also Armstrong's peer," Teachout writes. "Teagarden's easygoing way with a song complemented Armstrong instead of threatening him. If his chops were down, he could step aside and let Brother T drawl his way through "Stars Fell on Alabama."

The one time Armstrong did take a strong stand on racism was in 1957, when he condemned President Eisenhower and Alabama Governor Faubus for the way blacks were being treated in the South. His statements may have prompted Eisenhower to take action in a desegregation case, because soon after Armstrong made them, he ordered blacks to be admitted to Little Rock's Central High School, which prompted a congratulatory telegram to the President from Armstrong.

Pops chronicles Armstrong's life from childhood, when he was sentenced to a term in the Colored Waif's Home in New Orleans for firing a pistol on New Year's Eve, to the end of his life, when he lived comfortably in a large house in Queens with his fourth wife, Lucille. Among the highlights of the book are recognitions of a number of firsts Armstrong achieved: Swing That Music was the first autobiography to be written by a jazz musician. Armstrong was the first jazz musician to appear on the cover of Time magazine. He was the first black to host his own network radio variety show.

He moved from New Orleans to Chicago, Chicago to New York, spent time in California, and traveled with his band throughout Europe. The book contains a number of performance and personal pictures, from King Oliver's Creole jazz band in 1923, with Armstrong playing next to his second wife, Lil Hardin, the band's pianist, to Armstrong seated at a desk in his home in Queens in 1958, typing. Armstrong was quite prolific, having written two autobiographies, as well as numerous articles for national publications.

There are many other biographies and autobiographies of Armstrong. Teachout's stands out for its use of so many sources, its frequent quotes of Armstrong, the musicians he played with, and the critics who analyzed his work. Pops is an attempt to present a comprehensive view of Armstrong's life, not all of it terribly positive.

Yes, Armstrong's music was watered down, and yes, he was overly accommodating to whites, but in the end, he was a highly affable and talented man, who never stopped working, creating his own brand of music based on the original jazz that flourished in his native New Orleans, and popularizing it from coast to coast during his entire lifetime.

Harry Belafonte—My Song (A Memoir)

With Michael Shnayerson

Alfred A. Knopf | 469 pages | $30.50

Reviewed by Herb Boyd

Harry Balafonte
Credit: Pamela Belafonte

My first encounter with Harry Belafonte occurred as a teenager when his "Day-O" and "Jamaica Farewell" were at the top of the charts and calypso was all the rage. I had a friend who was so absolutely fascinated by Belafonte; he did everything to be like him, including his dress, mannerisms, and hair-style. We used to kid him that it was too bad he couldn't sing because otherwise he was a dead ringer.

For years the world has been waiting for Harry Belafonte to tell his story, to sing a song of his life that only he could do. Often when reporters asked about the possibility of such a memoir or autobiography, Belafonte would quickly brush off the inquiry, insisting they move on to the next question.

Many were left to conclude that maybe he had too many skeletons in the closet, too many things about him he'd rather not discuss, incidents and episodes he'd rather not relive.

Well, those skeletons and episodes come fully to life in *My Song*, and the legendary singer/actor/activist spills out his story, warts and all.

Readers finally get the lowdown about his off-and-on friendship with Bill Cosby and Sidney Poitier, whom he met when both were aspiring actors at the American Negro Theatre in Harlem; in jarring detail you learn of his love affairs and the circumstances that ended his two marriages, his infatuation with the doomed Dorothy Dandridge; his falling out with the King family to whom he devoted such love and affection, and there's even the revelation about a mole from the FBI who manipulated his way into Belafonte's trust.

Rewarding, too, are his unsparing impressions of President Obama, who in his estimation "seems to lack a fundamental empathy with the dispossessed, be they black or white." And there's more.

These are just a few of the titillating moments in a lengthy book stocked with two sections of photographs from his glorious career.

My Song is split between Belafonte the actor and Belafonte the activist, and even some of his most ardent fans may be surprised anew to know just how much of his time, energy and money were given over to civil and human rights struggles.

Given his matchless sacrifices—and risks—you would have to be completely heartless not to cut him some slack for all his indiscretions and dalliances.

Among Belafonte's idols were Paul Robeson ("he gave me my epiphany"), and to a great degree he's patterned his life after the immortal Robeson, rarely ever comprising his artistic and political integrity. In fact, Belafonte's art and politics are so tightly interwoven that they are as immutably consistent and unimpeachable as they are inseparably joined.

It isn't easy to find one passage that summarizes his steadfast conviction and unwavering commitment to freedom, justice and equality, but this one may be serviceable: "Race was the cutting edge in everything I did," he said about his role as a black entertainer. "To let myself be turned into an object of ridicule would undermine not just my stage persona, but my purpose as well."

***

Thanks to HBO, folks have seen the documentary of Belafonte's odyssey, but that's just a trailer, and it comes nowhere near delivering the juicy details that populate each page of this book. Yes, there are a few false steps and miscues that a discerning Black historian and Harlemite would have caught, but they are minor and forgivable.

Belafonte, now a bald-headed octogenarian with a new wife, is still a captivating American icon, though his stripped vocal cords have put an end to his concert days.

In place of his raspy voice, there's *My Song*, and in so many warm and wonderful ways it's really *our song*.

Too Smart for His Own Good
Malcolm X: A Life of Reinvention

by Manning Marable
Viking | 2011 | 594 pages

Reviewed by Fred Beauford

"To be a Negro living in America, and to be consciously aware, is to be in a state of constant outrage."

James Baldwin

As I look back on the history of this country, no one fits Baldwin's observation better than Malcolm Little (aka Malcolm X).

As he slowly emerges in Manning Marable's sometimes overwhelming, richly researched, 594 page book, he is an often perplexing combination of incredibly high intelligence, abject ignorance, a profound awareness and an unbending anger at America's mistreatment of blacks; all of which guide him, and tears him apart, leading him to become one of the most famous of Americans, the angry, revenge seeking Malcolm X.

The seeds for this transformation, which Professor Marable outlines with considerable skill and scholarship--were planted early.

Both of Malcolm's parents were dedicated followers of the Jamaican immigrant, Marcus Garvey. Professor Marable points out that Garvey and his followers believed that "Racial separation…was essential…people of African descent were all part of a transnational "nation." A global race with a common destiny."

This was during the time that one of the greatest human migrations in modern history was set into motion, as blacks started fleeing the fascist south, first in small trickles, and then in droves, in search of the democracy they had heard so much about.

Also, something just as motivating and whose importance continues until this day, was buried deep in Malcolm's parents' psyche, as well as most African Americans:

Who am I? Who was I before I was dragged unwillingly to this horrendous place called America?

Newly formed black communities in the urban north, in

cities like Detroit, New York's Harlem, Cleveland and Chicago, were rife with exploitative religious charlatans and deeply sincere individuals like Garvey, all with the same compelling answer to the confused blacks trying mightily to find an answer to the two tormenting, overwhelming questions that constantly haunted them: you are not who the slave master said you were and here is who you really are.

Malcolm's father, Earl Little, and his second wife Louise, Malcolm's mother, threw themselves into Garvey's organization, the Universal Negro Improvement Association (UNIA).

***

Malcolm's mother grew up in St. Andrew, Grenada. His dark-skinned, American born father lived most of his life in the Great Lakes region, the Midwest and even Canada, where he first met Malcolm's mother.

“Unlike Earl,” writes Marable, “she had received an excellent Anglican elementary-level education, becoming a capable writer as well as fluent in French…had a fair complexion and dark, flowing hair; in everyday encounters she was often mistaken for white.”

Despite such strong differences in background and physical appearances, what united them was a passionate commitment to Garvey’s famous dictum: “Up you mighty race. You can be what you will!”

Misfortune soon overwhelmed Malcolm’s family, however, and the bare outline of what happened next has been well documented, with additional, tantalizing and controversial nuggets sprinkled throughout the narrative of Professor Marable’s biography.

After the suspicious death of his father, his mother confined to a mental hospital, foster homes, crime, jail; and ultimately, the Nation of Islam, led by Elijah Muhammad, Malcolm Little finally becomes Malcolm X.

It was here, as a young, uneducated man in his twenties, that his barely noticed towering intellect, and his inner self-discipline, came to center stage. As an organizer, public speaker and debater, Malcolm X excelled and began to attract much attention, including local police, as well as the Feds, and he soon began to be watched wherever he went.

Although he knew the FBI was on his tail, this did nothing to deter him, and he kept up a punishing schedule, traveling to Los Angeles, to Detroit, to Chicago, and to Boston, all the while serving as the Minster of the Harlem temple.

Marable points out that, "Although Malcolm usually spoke at Muslim temples (later changed to mosque after growing heat from orthodox Muslin). his audiences increasingly consisted of both Muslim and non-Muslim blacks. In his language and style, Malcolm reached out to recruit black Christians to his cause."

His growing popularity "generated a financial windfall for the Nation. Between five hundred and one thousand African Americans were joining almost every month…much of the new revenue went into commercial ventures…the economic success of these ventures may have been responsible for Elijah Muhammad's decision to stop mentioning some of the original tenets of Wallace D. Fard's Islam—in particular the bizarre Yacub's history—and give greater emphasis to the Garveyite thesis that a self-sustainable, all-black capitalist economy was a viable strategy," writes Professor Marable.

Malcolm X was blessed with a trademark "bitter wit," and was a powerful public speaker (How many books I have read that pointed out that the real history of us humans is how we react to the spoken word. It seems that the speech is mightier than the pen, or the sword).

Media and universities, including Howard, Cornell and Harvard soon sought him out to speak before students and faculty, or provide a quote. This interest was fueled by the very real drama of the growing Civil Rights Movement in the south.

They all knew by now, that Malcolm was a great orator, and a provocative and confident lecturer.

Combined with the television screen suddenly being filled with brilliant black thinkers like James Baldwin, Bayard Ruskin, and now this guy who called himself Malcolm X, it provided an interesting, intellectual public face to the African American struggle, with more than merely black clerics from the south having visibility and the only voice.

It is easy to see, in the 20/20 hindsight of history, why he was in such demand.

Malcolm X would perhaps turn over in his grave at my

reference to his being an intellectual, but how else to account for the rapid learning experiences he had to face and master, time after time?

Herb Boyd points out, in his insightful review of the book in the *Amsterdam News,* that “It wasn’t a reinvention; rather an evolution.”

***

You hardcore eggheads out there reading this, please hold your nose, and forgive me, but reading this book brought back to mind an old *Star Trek* episode. In it, Captain Kirk is put on a strange planet, the likes of which he had rarely encountered, with a far greater physical reptilian adversary, by forces unknown.

The unknowns explained to both of them that everything they needed to defeat one another was right in front of them.

Captain Kirk, as well as Malcolm X, were both forced to quickly make use of whatever they found immediately around them; and their intelligence, and quick thinking were their main weapons against their opponents.

Kirk survived because of his intensive back knowledge, and even sternly lectured the powerful unknowns who had placed him there in the first place.

For Malcolm X, we all know what happened next. He did not survive, because he had little back knowledge when he embarked upon a journey that made him one of the most recognizable names to come out of the long struggle for freedom for African Americans.

He had to learn everything he needed to rise to such heights, as he went along in his remarkable journey.

His early ignorance, in spite of his being smart, ultimately caused jealousy and hatred and leading him down and trapped in a world that finally caught up with him, and bit him.

To me, this explains Malcolm X, and why, in the end, he just may have been too smart for his own good.

***

Another note concerning Malcolm X: Gene Roberts, the undercover NYPD officer that had infiltrated his organization and tried to revive him after he was shot down before his wife and children, was once a friend of mine, and one of the few black students at Olinville Junior High, and grew up near me in the Gunhill Houses.

***

Professor Manning Marable, a longtime member of the faculty of Columbia University, died the same day that his book, *Malcolm X: A Life of Reinvention* was released.

We all must go sometime, but I can't think of a better way to do it. This is a great book.

Roy Wilkins: The Quiet Revolutionary And The NAACP

By Yvonne Ryan

University Press of Kentucky | 285 pages

Reviewed by Robert Fleming

Of all of the key figures in the 1960s civil rights campaigns, Roy Ottoway Wilkins, the leader of the National Association for the Advancement of Colored People (NAACP), was not as popular as some of the warriors in the fight for equality. His low-key persona, coupled with his natural ability to work behind the scenes with elected officials in Washington, kept him out of the national spotlight, while more strident, militant voices hogged the attention of the media.

Yvonne Ryan, the managing editor of *The Economist's* annual *World In* publication, details the life and career of Wilkins, the cool and calm elder statesman, who served forty-four years with NAACP as an essential part of the team which achieved significant legislation, including the Civil Rights Act of 1965 and the Voting Rights Act of 1964.

This is the first biography of the rational, pragmatic, and tireless Wilkins (1901-1981) and one wonders why it has taken so long to document his man's achievements.

A native of St. Louis, Missouri, Wilkins was born on August 30, 1901 to a proud black family; his grandfather,

Asberry Wilkins, was a slave who won his freedom when he was fourteen years old.

Roy's father, William, was the second eldest of five children. Tragedy struck Roy's mother, Mayfield, who died of tuberculosis, but she wrote a letter to her sister, Elizabeth, before her death, asking for permission to move her young son to St. Paul, Minnesota.

His early years were spent in a modest home of his aunt in a low income, integrated community there.

His college life was marred with a brutal act of white prejudice. On June 15, 1920, three young black men, driving in Duluth, Minnesota, were accused of raping a white woman. Police evidence gathered in the case stated the trio was a part of a six-man gang involved in the deed.

Shortly after their incarceration, a bitter white mob rushed the jail, grabbed the black youths, convicted them in a bogus trial, and hanged them. This was a cruel emotional slap to young Wilkins' head because he had never witnessed a hanging, which was very common in the South.

Although Wilkins would later be labeled a moderate, that vigilante spirit engulfing the white mob put him to some realizations. "For the first time in my life, I understood what Du Bois had been writing about," he recalled of the incident. "I found myself thinking of black people as a very vulnerable *us* – and white people as an unpredictable violent *them.*"

Once Wilkins entered the University of Minnesota, he was determined to make a difference. He graduated with a degree in sociology in 1923. The writing bug bit him hard, allowing him to write on social and racial issues, as he became the first black reporter on *The Minnesota Daily* and later became editor of *St. Paul Appeal*, a black newspaper with a historic tradition on being on the right side of things.

His father notified him of an opportunity as the editor of *The Kansas City Call*, and his first plum assignment, was the coverage of the NAACP Annual National Convention, this year held in Kansas City. This launched him in certain circles of the Association's most influential officials.

Wilkins was very proud that he peddled copies of *The Crisis*, the Association's publication, as a boy. At age twenty-two, he served as a secretary at the St. Paul branch of the NAACP, and later assumed the same post at the Kansas City organization. Under his leadership, Wilkins undercut the nomination of Judge John Parker to the Supreme Court, declaring the jurist of making racist remarks. The young secretary wielded a blow-torch approach in his *Call* column to make the public take a second closer look at the bigoted candidate. He waged a similar battle against another conservative, Kansas senator Henry Allen, turning the tide to the victor, George McGill, a Democrat.

Officials at the NAACP paid attention to the triumphs of the young man from the Kansas City office. Walter White, the Association's assistant secretary, thought Wilkins had the goods, and a friendship developed between them. Armed with a sense of the organization's historic watchdog past, Wilkins recognized they knew his skill as a motivator, and understanding he was a man who could get things done.

In 1930, W. E. B. Du Bois asked Wilkins to join the NAACP national staff as the business manager of *The Crisis,* wanting to get some fresh blood in the front offices of the Association.

Beyond the new opportunities involving work, there was a private Roy Wilkins, and matters of intimacy and the heart could be as tangled and complicated as the betrayals and infighting he would endure in the NAACP turf war. He had a brother, Earl, who he once hired as an advertising salesman at *The Call*, an emotional pairing so deep that they even dated sisters. Wilkins thought about marrying Marvel Jackson, a college acquaintance, and Earl swept her sister, Helen, off her feet and to the altar.

Meanwhile, Marvel moved to New York to work on the staff of *The Call*, then to *The Amsterdam News,* involving in the whirlwind of the Big City's social life. Though she and Wilkins planned to wed, he met Aminda Badeau, a social worker and a recent St. Louis refugee. Later, Wilkins wrote a letter to his beloved which said he had got Badeau pregnant and pledged to remedy the situation. That suited everybody, for Marvel broke off the engagement and Wilkins married Badeau in 1929. However, his family suspected the woman fooled him, because there were no children born to the couple who remained married to her 1981 death.

At this point, the NAACP organization was in turmoil, pitting the administrators and workers into a conflict between the warring camps of Dr. Du Bois and Walter White, over tactics and expenditures. In December 1931, the split worsened and a move was made to oust White with a Du Bois memo to the National Board of Director of the organization, complaining of his rival's ineffectiveness in his post. Wilkins signed the memo, along with three of his colleagues. The ill-conceived power play fizzled when the Association's president, Joel Spingarn, agreed to investigate the allegations lodged against White and Mary White Ovington, its chairman and founder.

The book's author, Ryan, skillfully handles the inner struggles of the Association, choosing not to avoid the trash talk, backbiting, and plotting of Du Bois and White. She talks about the successes of the early group, such as monitoring the pay and treatment of black workers working on federally levee programs in Mississippi and Louisiana. Ryan also explains how the NAACP was too timid to take the lead in the 1931 Scottsboro Boys case, where nine black youths were charged with the rape of two white women on a freight train.

Despite some major skirmishes inside the Association during the 1940s , the organization maintained its mandate to defeat discrimination in the US military, war factories, and municipal housing. The opponents of the NAACP accused it of hypocrisy for pushing black men to fight for the country while being refused citizenship on its shores.

With the cooperation of the NAAC , A. Philip Randolph, leader of the Brotherhood of Sleeping Car Porters, demanded a March on Washington to protest bias in the war industries and in the armed services.

President Roosevelt saw the planned march as a loaded gun in the tentative calm of the nation's capital and signed Executive Order 8802, creating a federal committee to end the prejudice in the defense industry and government.

The book chronicles both the minor and major triumphs in the NAACP career of Wilkins, such as the founding of the Leadership Conference on Civil Rights (LCCR), by the Association executive, Randolph and Jewish leader Arnold Aronson in 1950, and the 1954 Supreme Court landmark decision in the *Brown vs. Board of Education*, outlawing racially segregated public schools. The following year, NAACP worked with those who wanted to bring to justice to the killers of Emmett Till, the 14-year-old Chicago black youth beaten to death for allegedly whistling at a white woman in Mississippi.

While Rev. King's rise to prominence in the civil rights campaign is noted in Roy Wilkins: The Quiet Revolutionary And The NAACP, the author returns again and again to the public and private feud between the Nobel Prize-winning minister and Wilkins, due to their personal styles.

Rev. King could read the Yellow Pages with gospel gusto

and drive a crowd into a frenzy, while Wilkins put the listeners to sleep with his polite, mannered oratory. At every significant event during the 1960s in the long road to equality, the two men took notice of the other, and jockeyed for media attention at the 1963 March on Washington, the 1965 Selma to Montgomery marches, and the 1966 March Against Fear.

Often, Wilkins was the centerpiece of any civil rights effort to influence elected officials in Washington, because they could deal with his moderate tone rather than hot head militants like H. Rap Brown or Stokely Carmichael. In 1967, he was presented with the Presidential Medal of Freedom by President Johnson. Being an elder statesman from another era, he was ridiculed as an Uncle Tom and a tool of Capitol Hill. Even the young lions of the NAACP rose up against him repeatedly, but he usually outfoxed them until his retirement in 1977 at age 76. The leadership was taken over by

Benjamin Hooks.

A year after he left the NAACP, the media accused him of collaborating with the FBI to discredit Rev. King, which he denied. Wilkins died September 9, 1981.

What distinguishes this biography from many of those civil rights warriors is Ryan's supreme skill at not letting any negative rumors or allegations hijack the memorable achievements of Roy Wilkins. She elevates the life of this disciplined, dignified, complex soul. Wonderfully written and illuminating, this book celebrates a very private man operating in tense public situations under the microscope of the media.

Booker T. Washington Rediscovered

Edited by Michael Scott Bieze and Marybeth Gasman

The John Hopkins University Press | 2012

Reviewed by Fred Beauford

"Cast down your bucket where you are." Booker T.

Washington, 1895, in a speech before the Cotton States and International Exposition in Atlanta.

Once, when I was an undergraduate at New York University, I participated in a public debate. The question on the floor: Resolve, who was right, Booker T. Washington or Dr. W.E.B. Du Bois in regard to which direction Negroes should go?

Since I organized the debate, I assigned myself the role of Booker T. Washington, the second ever nationally known black leader in America, following in the giant footsteps of Frederick Douglass, and who has been called a founding father of African American education in the United States because he founded the famed Tuskegee Normal and Industrial Institute in 1891.

***

To this day, I am convinced that I could have won that

debate if my opponent hadn't gone Baptist Minister, and stomped all over me.

He quickly took over, and soon had the crowd in an uproar. My cool, impeccable logic meant little here.

Still, for most of my adult life, Booker T. Washington's main message has stayed with me: blacks needed to keep producing things, like they were once forced to do in slavery; and now make it work for them. I chose to take the role of Washington in that debate because I had felt that Booker T. and I had reached the same conclusion: it was for very real reasons that black slaves were the most valuable people in the new world.

***

Booker T. Washington Rediscovered is a very interesting way to present both the ideas and the man behind them: a mixed race ex-slave, who rose to become one of the most important figures in American life, and his fame became worldwide.

His book *Up from Slavery*, first published in 1901, has never gone out of print.

***

"In 1895," writes the online site historymatters.gmu.edu, "Booker T. Washington gave what later came to be known as the Atlanta Compromise speech before the Cotton States and International Exposition in Atlanta. His address was one of the most important and influential speeches in American history, guiding African-American resistance to white discrimination and establishing Washington as one of the leading black spokesmen in America. Washington's speech stressed accommodation rather than resistance to the racist order under which Southern African Americans lived. In 1903, Washington recorded this portion of his famous speech, the only surviving recording of his voice."

Washington's many distracters, especially Dr. Du Bois, often cite this speech as proof that he had become the dreaded Uncle Tom, the turn coat, the sell-out, the person all African Americans have been taught, for good reasons, for generations, to hate and despised, even more than the Northern European settlers.

***

We have none of this in *Booker T. Washington Rediscovered*. We meet Booker T. Washington by the many magazine articles he wrote, all in their original, printed form, typos and all; and the many speeches he gave.

"Booker T. Washington," the editors write, "was once one of the Progressive Age's most popular speakers on both sides of the color line. His public speaking gift first received acclaim when a *New York Times* reporter mentioned the young Washington's skill in an article, after hearing Washington speak at his 1875 Hampton Institute graduation. Debating and public speaking became his passion."

As I read this, I once more marveled at the role great public speaking has played in human history. To repeat myself, the speech, it seems, has always been more compelling than either the pen, or the sword.

***

I would recommend this book to those who may have heard of the famed "Wizard of Tuskegee," but know little of what he stood for. With *Booker T. Washington Rediscovered*, we hear directly from him, with no historians, or political types with an ax to grind, or even being celebratory, weighing in.

Booker T. Washington was once one of the most famous persons in the world. The school he founded still educates scores of black people, both men and women. And it has served a great need, welcoming everyone from newly freed slaves, to the famous Tuskegee Airmen of World War Two.

Singer/songwriter Lionel Richie grew up on the campus of Tuskegee; his grandfather's house was right across the street from the home of the president of the college. It was there, later as a student, that he helps form The Commodores, who went on to have many national hit records.

Richie became a single act as a singer/songwriter, and has had much success. But he is not done. In what is an excellent love kiss to the school, the region, and the kinds of music it produced, Richie has given us what I think is the CD of 2012, *Tuskegee.*

***

I know personally, if I knew little about someone like

Booker T. Washington, I would want to know more, and this book would be a great place to start.

Harlem's Rattlers and the Great War: The Undaunted 369th Regiment and the African American Quest for Equality

By Jeffrey T. Sammons and John H. Morrow, Jr.

University Press of Kansas | 2014

Reviewed by Brenda M. Greene

Jeffery Sammons

Harlem Goes to War

This comprehensive and in-depth study, with photos, extensive notes and biographical references was written over a ten-year period. It provides the reader with an additional lens by which to view the legacy of Harlem's Rattlers. It is a book that readers of military history will cherish and that general readers and lovers of history will find informative. It is both a reference book and an important historical narrative that lays the ground for the civil rights movement.

At a recent forum on *Harlem's Rattlers and the Great War* at Medgar Evers College, Sammons began his presentation by describing how the story of the Black soldiers who served in this unit was a testimony to the character of these men:

He told the audience “that it is character, not reputation that determines your place in history and the legacy which you will leave. If these men had been dependent on the reputation by which they were labeled, they would have never formed the unit that marked them in history. Their character speaks loudly in this important study of the “Undaunted 369th Regimentime

The rattler, distinguished by its rattle and considered aggressive, a deadly foe and natural predator, uses it venom to strike at internal forces within its own environment and when it perceives a threat, will strike at external forces it encounters. This book chronicles the history of the 369th Regiment, the original 15th Regiment of Black soldiers who fought in France during World War I.

The rattler became the insignia of this unit as evidenced by its image on the Commemorative Firsts History Proclamation of the 15th New York Colored Infantry and the 369th Infantry. This proclamation was presented to Colonel Benjamin O. Davis, Commanding Officer of the 369th Infantry, on June 23rd 1939.

One of the longest serving infantry combat units on the front line (191 days in France) theirs was known as a unit that never lost a soldier to capture or a foot of the ground it had captured. Although this Regiment, which earned the Croix de Guerre, is more commonly known as *Harlem's Hellfighters*, Sammons and Morrow, deliberately choose not to use this name which they suggest was made popular by the media.

They inform us that this name, never embraced by the unit itself, limits the entire narrative behind Harlem's Rattlers. Sammons and Morrow have chosen to expand this comprehensive narrative of Harlem's Rattlers by giving the back story leading up to the legislation that legitimatized the formation of the 369th Infantry Regiment (formerly known as the 15th New York National Guard Regiment), the post-war challenges faced by the unit after its return from France, and the current state of the 369th Unit.

Sammons and Morrow have done an extraordinary job in conveying the complex narrative of the men who dared to resist and to demand a valued place for their participation in WWI. When initially approached to write the story of Harlem's Rattlers, Sammons enlisted the partnership of his colleague Morrow, a leading military historian of World War I with fluency in French and German who had great familiarity with the records of the 369th Regiment.

The resulting 500-page book of military history provides a sociological and political context in which the highly charged drama of the 369th unfolds. The writers describe the city, state and national politics surrounding the formation of the 369th Regiment and the many obstacles faced by the men, soldiers and leaders who advocate for a Black combat infantry regiment.

The book begins and opens with a description of Henry Lincoln Johnson, the first combat hero of the 369th Regiment, who is most closely identified with the regiment. When warned to retreat by a white French lieutenant in 1918 France, Johnson responds, "I am an American and I never retreat." Johnson's words underscore the impact of this experience for those who chose to fight in a Black regiment of the New York National Guard; there was hope that this fight for democracy on foreign soil would result in an affirmation of respect for Black Americans. This was a fight for civil rights and social justice, for manhood in a gendered society, for equal participation in a democracy, and for the freedom that should have been afforded all Americans.

Johnson's declaration of himself as an American who never retreats underscores the irony faced by those in the 369th Regiment. The paradox of going to their possible death in France while facing bigotry and prejudice in America cannot be underscored. Sammons and Morrow note that the scholar Richard Slotkin correctly labels the Regiment's "transfer to the French army, "a liberation rather than an exile."

The representation of historical events in film and literature never become visible in a vacuum. Sammons and Morrow illustrate this by providing the cultural and political context in which the story of the 369th Regiment emerged in popular culture. Almost 25 years after the original 369th had returned from WWI, the 369th, after serving in the Pacific during WWII, returned to New York in 1943. Like the soldiers of the original 369th Unit, they participated in an historic march up Fifth Avenue.

Sammons and Morrow offer critical commentary on the launching of the classic film *Stormy Weather* at this time. Racial tension and discrimination were intense; riots had erupted in Detroit, Harlem and Los Angeles. And Civil Rights leaders were pressuring Hollywood to employ more African Americans in less stereotypical and restrictive roles. Their critique of *Stormy Weather* focuses on the ways in which the contributions of Black soldiers were misrepresented and diminished in the film; for example, there is an implication that Bojangles Robinson, a central character in the film, was actually part of the 369th Regiment. The truth is that Robinson never served in the regiment. Thus, viewers of the film can come away from it with inaccurate information, with the perception that Black soldiers played a minimal role in France during WWI, and with a narrow and superficial rendering of which Black soldiers were actually part of the 369th.

One might say that the film is successful because: it has a high cast of Black talents (Lena Horne, Fats Waller, Katherine Dunham, and Bojangles Robinson among others), is highly entertaining, and has extended reach. However, because the film is loosely based on characters in the 369th Regiment, Sammons and Morrow contend that the film is a disservice to the images of Blacks in WWI.

For example, the film refers to the 369th Regiment rather than the 15th Regiment; in omitting the name of the 15th Regiment, an important historical fact is inadvertently dismissed. Given that this popular film was a source of information on the Regiment (before this film, there had been only two dedicated treatments of the Regiment), Sammons and Morrow suggest that more could have been done to present an accurate portrayal of the Regiment. Moreover, because the band rather than the soldiers from the 369th Unit is highlighted in the film, it is not even clear that African Americans were actually part of a combat unit.

Throughout the book, Sammons and Morrow remind us that the very act of entering the military is and has been a gendered experience, one that is specifically significant for African American men who daily faced lynching and the discriminatory laws resulting from Jim Crow, and who were often a step away from dire poverty, high mortality rates, forced labor and continual attacks on their families.

For African American men, participation in the war also represented a symbolic affirmation of male masculinity and an act of resistance to the perpetuation of stereotypes of Black men as lazy, violent, dangerous, aggressive, angry and inferior.

A significant portion of the book is focused on detailing the politics and the racial climate behind the long struggle from a Provisional Regiment in 1911 to 1916 when the Regiment was formerly constituted in New York City. Republicans and whites attempted to delay the application of Black men, who were volunteers, not draftees, by establishing one unit at a time. One is surprised by some of the leaders who initially opposed the formation of the unit. W.E.B. DuBois, who was initially ambivalent about the unit, later encourages Blacks to join. A Philip Randolph questioned whether Blacks should fight this international war when they were facing injustice and racial discrimination at home.

Once formed, racism and efforts to deny the regiment full participation in the war continued. A Black unit was sent to the town of Spartanville, South Carolina and then to camps in Long Island and New Jersey where they faced hostility and rejection; they were even told not to retaliate. This was in response to the perception that there would be riots; the media also participated in perpetuating the myth that Black regiments would be harmful to the war effort. There was also a deliberate attempt to reject Black officers. The government placed inexperienced and less qualified white officers over experienced non-commissioned Black officers. This prolonged racism continued when the unit was initially sent overseas and although they had been trained for combat, they were relegated to serving as a labor battalion where they acted as stevedores, canal and ditch diggers until the French found it necessary to place them in combat.

Sammons and Morrow provide a comprehensive overview on the treatment of some of the soldiers upon their return to New York. The Regiment is disbanded. James Reese Europe, the band leader survives the war, but after achieving fame and performing a concert in Boston, Europe is fatally stabbed. Charles Ward Fillmore, who led the effort to form a Black regiment in the New York National Guard, should have had an opportunity to lead the unit. Like many other Blacks in the unit, he receives no American honors.

Horace Pippin, one of the non-commissioned officers and natural leaders, represents his wartime experience through his art. Noble Sissle, a member of Europe's Fifteenth Band and an advocate for the representation of Black performers on army bases and camps, was one of the Regiment's most important narrators. He is responsible for honoring the memory of General Gourard's Fourth French Army and his dear friend James Reese Europe. These people are but a few of the many who are part of the historical record of the 369th Regiment.

Atlas of the Transatlantic Slave Trade

by David Eltis and David Richardson

Yale University Press | 307 pages | $50.00

Reviewed by Loretta H. Campbell

The transatlantic slave trade built the wealth of Europe, certain African countries, and all of the Americas as outlined in the prodigious research of this book. Using 200 maps, it depicts 500 years of international trafficking in human beings. The information is separated into 6 parts (chapters) created and annotated by authors David Eltis (*The Rise of African Slavery in the Americas*) and David Richardson (director, Wilberforce Institute for the Study of Slavery and Emancipation). Both of these historians and scholars of African-American history also serve on the Electronic Slave Trade Datebase Project at Emory University.

The book immediately answers the question of why these Africans were enslaved. The answer is the greed of their captors. Precious minerals like gold and silver were mined in South America by Africans enslaved by the Spanish and Portugese. However, the minerals were eventually supplanted by the major drugs of the day: tobacco, coffee, rum, and sugar. Today's science has declared all of these products addictive. Certainly their addictive quality played a large part in consumer demand even at the cost of another's freedom or life.

Eltis and Richardson characterize this demand first in marketing terms: "...our Western culture tends to worship the magic of the free market, the invisible hand that allegedly promotes the common good."

However, that same adoration for capitalism had a tragic side. The authors continue, " Yet it was *uncontrolled* market forces that determined how many African slaves could be crammed into the hold of a ship--with the chained and padlocked males lying together for five weeks...surrounded by feces or urine drenched floors...to satisfy consumer demand for sugar, rum, tobacco, and coffee." Paintings and documents describe how food and water were so inadequate that sometimes captives starved to death with a matter of days.

Why or how did the enslavers come to believe it was

acceptable to subject other human beings to this kind of treatment? As the book elaborates, during the 1400s slavery became race based. According to the authors, racism ran deep and wide in most European countries. Darker skinned Europeans, Armenians, Italians, even Slavs (from which the word slave was produced) had been enslaved by lighter skinned Northern Europeans for centuries. However, only Africans or non-Europeans were enslaved to be shipped to the Americas.

The authors demonstrate how the most economically advanced European countries and the most agriculturally equipped African countries were involved in the trade first. The former countries bought the slaves; the latter countries supplied them. For Europeans, the slave trade was about profit. For the Africans (who were essentially selling their brothers and sisters), it was about profit, politics, and power. The victors in wars between linguistic groups enslaved the vanquished. Political rivals sold their competitors.

Eltis and Richardson don't shrink from exposing the culpability of Africans in the slave trade. In part III, there is a painting of *Gezo, King of Dahomey*, 1849. (Schomberg Center for Research in Black Culture, New York). In it, the king exemplifies the arrogance and cool brutality of African slavers. According to the legend under the picture, the slave trade flourished under his reign. In fact, his cruelty was on par with that of European slavers.

The painting *Slave Ship (Slavers Throwing Overboard the Dead and Dying, Typhoon Coming On),* shows the killing of 132 Africans. The rationale of the ship's captain was killing the Africans would enable the vessel to weather the storm. The ships's officers expected their loss to be covered by insurance.

Insurance companies and other businesses prospered as a result of the slave trade. There were companies that specialized in selling slaves, and companies that specialized in selling branding irons. In one picture, there is a branding iron with a small heart on it as if the future owner wants the slave to feel loved.

Yet, there was resistance by the captives themselves. The book details "patterns of slave resistance." The majority of revolts happened close to the western coast line.

"By capt. *[sic]* Wright of the Endeavour, from the Coast of Guinea, we had the following account of the loss of the Marlborough, capt. Codd, of Brtistol, by an insurrection of the Negroes the beginning of October last [1752]...,while most o fthe crew were below cleaning the rooms, and none but the captain and two white men, armed with cutlasses, left above to take care of the ship, all of a sudden the Negroes on deck snatched the arms from them, wounded the captain, and forced him up the foreshrouds, where they shot him dead."

Often the organizers of these revolts were women. This was because women were not shackled as the men were. The book also mentions that African women were often raped by their captors. It can be inferred that, because the voyages were so long (two years in many cases), babies were born aboard ship. The subject for another book would be how these women fared during pregnancy, childbirth, and what happened to their babies.

The other resistance was the worldwide abolition movement. The painting of the *Zong* murders galvanized the British abolitionist movement. Although laws against slavery had some impact, nothing brought it to a halt like the abolitionist movement in Britain and the Civil War in America. After half a millennium, the transatlantic slave trade became reprehensible, even anathema in Europe, the Americas, and the United States.

The English lead this movement and had naval ships patrolling the high seas to rescue Africans and free them. Various European countries and America made it illegal to transport slaves.(Ironically, America didn't outlaw slavery *inside* the United States until after the Civil War.)

The British Government created a Court of Mixed Commission to try and to levy fines on all countries that engaged in the transatlantic slave trade. That government resettled captives in British owned colonies and also along the western coast of Africa and in the Americas. Although the intentions were good, there were tragic problems; thousands of Africans were recaptured by slavers who raided these settlements.

Exact, yet sensitive, the book lists the horrors of going into bondage. Worthy attention is paid to the Middle Passage. "The only food we had during the voyage was corn soaked and boiled. I cannot tell how long we were thus confined... a great many slaves died upon the passage," wrote Mahomah G. Baquaqua who published this account after he escaped from slavery. Many survivors or escapees published their experiences and spoke out against the trade.

Eltis and Robinson consider the Middle Passage a way to determine how slavery "restructured the populations of both the society of origin and the society of arrival." History records that entirely new cultures were created in the Americas. Conversely, it can be assumed that entire peoples were lost because of this slave trade. The authors supply ship manifests detailing the deaths and dying of captives during the Middle Passage. They also give an invaluable jewel, the website, www.slavevoyages.org, which documents 35,000 slave ship voyages.

To say the information compiled here is awe inspiring is to *almost* do it justice. Listed here are names of victims; where they were kidnapped; how many came from which country; which year; and lesson plans on how to teach on the transatlantic slave trade.

The book also lays the groundwork for reparations. Because of its copious statistics, it's possible to calculate the financial cost of slavery. For example, using the website, a reader can multiple the "cost" of a slave by the number of slaves sold in a country in a certain amount of time. Cost of slaves from various countries are listed in the maps also.

Theoretically, the transatlantic slave trade ended. However, in its aftermath came share cropping, segregation, and systemic racism. The descendants of the slaves that built the financial support of world powers have never received any of the profits made by their ancestors. This book will be a real boon to the reparations movement and an aid to quantifying what is owed.

A Law Professor Who Tells Tales

An Interview with Stephen Carter

By Herb Boyd

For many years after he wrote *Reflections of an Affirmative Action Baby*, (Basic, 1991) Stephen Carter was content to dash off an occasional article or op-ed piece and to devote time and attention to the classroom at Yale University where he has been a professor of law since 1982. But in 2003 Carter emerged with fanfare in the fictional realm with *The Emperor of Ocean Park*(Knopf, 2002) which meant that the midnight oil was illuminating more than torts. Four years later, the professor's second novel *New England White* (Knopf, 2007) is raking in the reviews, most of them quite favorable, though Carter says he doesn't read any of them. He said --Well, let's allow the lawyer to present his own case.

This interview was conducted at the offices of Random House in midtown Manhattan on June 21:

Herb Boyd: Can you talk about your family a bit?

Stephen Carter: My father [Lyle Carter] was a lawyer in Harlem for many years in the Fifties before departing for Washington, D.C., to work for the Kennedy and Johnson administrations. My grandfather, who was Lyle, Sr., was a dentist in Harlem. My parents lived on Jumel Terrace, and I lived as a child at 435 Convent Avenue.

HB: I think that's the Garrison Apartments where Adam Clayton Powell, Sr. once lived. It's a historic building just up the block from where Joe Louis and Rose Morgan used to live. I was struck by how often Harlem is mentioned in your latest novel.

SC: My next novel will be about Harlem in the 1950s. In fact, I have a scene that takes place at the Jumel Mansion. I was up there recently doing some research. I was born in Washington, D.C., but I spent the first seven years of my life in Harlem. I attended P.S. 129. We left Harlem in 1961.

HB: Stephen, do you have a particular audience in mind when you write your novels?

SC: I don't really, and people often ask me that. My aim is to reach as many readers as possible. As a novelist, I don't think you can spend too much time thinking about whom you're writing for. You just want to write a story that makes sense that entertains people, a story they enjoy reading. I have no message in mind, other than, 'Is the book going to be fun to read?'

HB: Your first novel The Emperor of Ocean Park shot right to the top of the charts. Who were the people who bought this book?

SC: I don't know. It sold a lot of copies, but I have no idea who bought it. But I hear from people all over the country who have read it. A friend of mine who was on vacation in Peru skiing said he ran into someone reading the book on the ski slopes.

HB: But given the size of the book, its length and the subject matter, I don't think it's the kind of book you'll see people, especially young Blacks reading on the subway…don't you think it's a bit intimidating for certain kind of readers?

SC: I know that it is. But I couldn't make it shorter because I had a story to tell and it took a lot of pages to do that. I do recognize that you sell more copies if the book is shorter and rather straightforward, but that's not the way I write.

HB: Has there been much feedback, reviews and such from African American reporters and critics?

SC: So far, there have been a few reviews, and I've heard that most of them like it. I doubt, however, if I'll hear from anyone who said they hated the book. But by and large, I don't read the reviews. I don't think it's a good idea to read your reviews. If they are bad reviews, they will ruin your day. If they are good ones, then you begin thinking how you might need to please that critic, in the same way, with your next book. So, I try not to read them.

HB: Do you write to please yourself?

SC: I think all writers write to please themselves first. You see, writing is a lonely business. But a writer who sells books has a public. So you have to write to please that public to some extent. My wife [Enola Aird] reads all of my work, and she is, by far, my most thoughtful and critical reader. She's a lawyer and a real good editor, and a tough critic who will tell me if something is good or bad. Her careful reading has made me a much better writer.

HB: Are there other readers whom you rely on for feedback and response?

SC: Not really. After my wife, there's my editor and a few close friends with whom I'll share the first draft. Even so, you can't write by committee.

HB: Let's back up a bit. Most of our readers perhaps first heard of you from your nonfiction book Reflections of an Affirmative Action Baby *then the next time they read about you, you're the recipient of a huge advance to write two novels. Can you fill in some of the moments between the nonfiction and the fiction?*

SC: That's a fair question. But the answer goes back a bit, because I've always wanted to write fiction. When I was a little boy in Washington, D.C., I would purchase those little spiral notebooks that cost a dime and I would fill them with my stories. There would be stories about dinosaurs taking over the earth, those kinds of childhood fantasies. The point is that I've always wanted to write. I'm not sure where that comes from. I wrote seven nonfiction books before I was able to get back to what I wanted to write all along. One of the things that helped me to get into fiction again was that I had characters that I wanted to write about., and with these characters in my head, I was just waiting for a story to come along…

HB: They were characters in search of a plot…

SC: Right. Most writers, I believe, start with a plot or a scene. But I think about characters and their relationship to each other, and that's what generates the story. In *The Emperor of Ocean Park*, I had in mind this Black judge who was involved in a mystery, and bit by bit his family suggested itself, his wife and circumstances came into play.

HB: Have you read much fiction over the years, and are you currently a reader of fiction?

SC: I've read fiction most of my life, but like a lot of fiction writers, I've read less fiction since I started writing it. It's hard to enjoy it as much. Now I tend to read it as a writer rather than as a reader. I read a book and think how I would have done it differently. So, that takes a lot of the fun out of it. Mainly, now, I read history, biographies, and some theology. Right now I'm reading a book by David Brion Davis on slavery.

HB: There's so much economic theory in New England White, so you must have boned up on that.

SC: I do a lot of research, which I don't mind doing since I like to have my facts straight. For example, I talk about antique mirrors in the book, and I didn't know anything at all about them, so I had to do some research. Antique mirrors are not a hobby of mine, but I had to learn about them. The parts [of the book] that I didn't make up, I like to have my facts accurate.

HB: Speaking of making it up, are there some famous Black writers you've read who influenced you?

SC: I usually stay away from talking about living writers because invariably someone will ask me why so and so wasn't mentioned. Now, James Baldwin is a writer I greatly admired. I was always struck by his characterizations. I really think his novel *Go Tell It on the Mountain* is one of the great novels of the Twentieth Century. And you can't help but to be influenced by Ralph Ellison, Richard Wright and Langston Hughes. Hughes had a remarkable ear for dialogue. Baldwin had this ability to bring about the power of emotion, and Ellison on the complexity of an individual's experience.

HB: I think your female readers are certainly going to appreciate how well you handled Mrs. Carlyle…

SC: I didn't start out to make a woman the main character. It just developed that way, she was so dominant. A lot of women who have read the book believe I've done a good job capturing her voice. And I hope that's right.

HB: *Two of your characters, Vanessa and Gina, and their relationship reminded me of the ghost elements in Toni Morrison's Beloved…*

SC: No one has pointed that out to me. I don't know if there are similarities. I read the book, but I didn't see the movie. The Toni Morrison book I like best is *Song of Solomon.*

HB: And the next novel, will it explore the lives of other characters who are only vaguely present in the current one?

SC: Well, let me say this, the next book will cover the period of the Fifties to the Seventies, and will include a lot more about Harlem.

HB: You've discussed a bit of your writing process, that it's done mostly in the morning at a computer with no set number of words to write per sitting. What advice do you have for that writer struggling to complete a project?

SC: I always tell my audience that a lot of people can write stories, but most people don't.Why? Well, you're not a real writer until you can say to people you like, whose company you enjoy, that you can't hang out that night -- that you have to write. You have to treat it like any other job. A lawyer can say he can't come to dinner tonight because he has a brief to write and [has] to be in court in the morning, and a doctor tells you she can't be at such and such place because she has to rest up for surgery, then you, as a writer, should be able to say the same about your craft. You have to take it seriously.

Herb Boyd is an author and senior editor of New World Review.

New England White

by Stephen L. Carter

$26.95, Hardcover, Knopf (June 20

Whither Black Intellectuals?

An essay by Herb Boyd

Jerry Gafio Watts

Nothing invigorates a debate about black intellectuals more than when they disagree among themselves, and their differences become grist for the media. A recent example of this war of words, a takedown in rhetoric occurred back in the spring when Michael Eric Dyson excoriated Cornel West, his former mentor.

Published in the *New Republic*, the blistering attack went viral all over the Internet, which was clearly part of the author's intentions. Interested parties waited eagerly for West's retort, but, for the most part, the pragmatic scholar was momentarily silent, choosing to let the verbal fusillade fade into the ether.

Toward the end of Dyson's screed, we get at least a glimmer of his motivation for the 10,000 word essay. For several months—if not years—the bile from West had accumulated, necessitating a release.

Dyson said West had assailed him with a barrage of disparaging comments, including that he was a "cheerleader and bootlicker" for President Obama. When West finally broke his silence, he said, "Character assassination is the refuge of those who hide and conceal these issues in order to rationalize their own allegiance to the status quo."

And thus the bout was on.

Students of African American history and intellectual thought probably heard a familiar ring in the encounter between these two very popular public intellectuals. In the distant black past, there was a similar rift—but far more political--in the abolitionist movement.

In 1843, the National Negro Convention was held in Buffalo, New York. Among the delegates was the Rev. Henry Highland Garnet and the meeting would have long been forgotten except for his speech that called for slave rebellions. His position was opposed by Frederick Douglass, who preferred a less militant approach to eradicating slavery.

"Let your motto be resistance," Garnet bellowed. He fell one vote shy of commanding the day.

A few years later, Douglass, the leading black intellectual of the era, would disagree with Martin Delany about the role of white abolitionists in the movement. Douglass was a consistent proponent of moral suasion, which put him at odds with the more radical and militant plans of John Brown, though aligned with Wendell Phillips and William Lloyd Garrison.

For Delany, the white abolitionists were prejudiced and he insisted that blacks help themselves.

This split put an end to the working relationship between the two thinkers who had combined their energy and insight in publishing the *North Star*. They personified the growing ideological and philosophical divide in the black community, a fissure that would become wider with the arrival of W.E.B. Du Bois and Booker T. Washington.

It seems to me, said Booker T, I don't agree, said W.E.B." is a line from a poem by Dudley Randall and it encapsulates the differing outlooks of the two great men. Many books have been written about their argument over the best route to citizenship and liberty for black Americans. Both Washington and Du Bois were vying for the leadership of their people after the death of Douglass in 1895. At one time there was a chance for them to fuse their outlooks but that vanished when Washington's accommodationist views clashed with Du Bois' determined push for full civil rights.

Their disagreement was never as rancorous and bitter as the one Du Bois would have with Washington's successor, in effect, Marcus Garvey. Despite their common Pan-Africanist perspectives, they could not overcome the personal dislike that festered with each intemperate published comment. Their dispute was soon the source of an ongoing feud that nullified the possibility of any unity in the black community.

Interestingly, Ida B. Wells and Mary Church Terrell stood apart from the ground forged by them, establishing their own independent ideas about race relations and human rights.

***

The delightful and pleasant veneer of the Harlem Renaissance often concealed the perturbations among some of the artistic denizens. A bit of a rumble from some of the leading thinkers occurred over their stance on white author Carl Van Vechten's novel*Nigger Heaven (*Alfred A. Knopf, 1926*)*.

To some degree it was reminiscent of the problems during the abolitionist phase and how to deal with whites who had insinuated themselves into the ranks. But this proved to be a minor disturbance compared to the disgust brewed by Langston Hughes and Zora Neale Hurston over their play "Mule Bone." At the heart of the issue was which of the writers rightfully owned the work and who could curry the favor of their benefactor, a white woman.

When James Baldwin lacerated Richard Wright in his earliest essays, many recognized a traditional skirmish that pitted one black intellectual against another. Baldwin's challenge to Wright had territorial aspects, very much like his critique of Hughes over the turf in Harlem, but it was basically one of literary form and content. While it never degenerated into a nasty back-and-forth, it was clearly adversarial and competitive, and a quarrel that would, circumstantially, include Ralph Ellison.

Ellison's presence loomed recently with the death of Jerry Watts. The title of Watts's book *Heroism & The Black Intellectual—Ralph Ellison, Politics, and Afro-American Intellectual Life (*University of North Carolina Press, 1994*)*, indicates his path and admiration of Ellison, who, "of all major contemporary black intellectual figures…probably comes least to mind when we think of politically engaged intellectuals," he mused.

Ellison, thus, represents the politically conscious intellectual intent on reflecting about "their duties, allegiances, and ambitions." Watts' evaluation of Baldwin is not comforting, dismissing him as a "black victim-status intellectual."

In his baleful hook no one but Ellison is spared. His estimation of Harold Cruse whose *The Crisis of the Negro Intellectual* (Quill, 1994) sparked a longstanding discussion, Watts opines, that he interpreted "the history of twentieth century Afro-American intellectuals through a lens of dogmatic ideology."

Later, in an article he wrote for *Dissent*, Watts was even self-condemnatory. "While I have some contributions to make to the betterment of black life, I can easily understand the low priority that many blacks give to my situation as an anxiety-ridden bourgeois black academic intellectual."

At his funeral this year on Dec. 5, as expected there was a large gathering of black and white intellectuals at the New York Society for Ethical Culture. Right down front, his head tilted back and his afro visible from any angle was Dr. Cornel West.

In his book, Watts took West to task for his inclusion of some entertainers in the Black intellectual tradition. In a footnote, he observed "Certainly, jazz vocalists and preachers are linked to traditions, but they are not for the most part linked to intellectual traditions."

During his speeches, West often invokes the jazz immortal John Coltrane and James Brown. This critique was probably impervious to West whose blurb cited the book as "superb."

***

The evolution of black intellectual thought turned very political, at least publicly in the fifties as the civil rights movement took shape with a certain amount of intensity fomented by Dr. Martin Luther King, Jr. and Adam Clayton Powell, Jr.

Concomitant to their outbursts--one centered on who wore the crown--was the emergence of the Nation of Islam, and its most iconic figures, Elijah Muhammad and Malcolm X. In a very short period, their presumed alliance ruptured acrimoniously, ending in a fatalistic hatred.

Before his assassination Malcolm was on a fast track to international acclaim, gradually setting aside his denouncements of King and other civil rights leaders.

Even so, the residue from the previous generation of antagonism found resonance in the Black Panther Party. When Huey Newton and Eldridge Cleaver went their separate radical ways they merely circled back on each other, inviting their acolytes to a deadly internecine warfare. One of the promising moments of these halcyon days was the temporary merger of the Panthers with some former members of the Student Nonviolent Coordinating Committee, principally Stokely Carmichael (Kwame Ture), H. Rap Brown, and James Forman. The marriage was irreconcilable.

As mentioned earlier, black intellectual thought was quite vibrant in the sixties, particularly as manifested in the plays, poetry, and artistic expressions evinced by a number of groups and formations. Amiri Baraka represented the quintessential Black Nationalist before diverging into Marxist-Leninism. Soon it was a standoff that one wag termed a contest between "the narrow nationalists and the mechanical Marxists."

Baraka's sudden departure from a coterie that included Haki Madhubuti, Dr. John Henrik Clarke, Chancellor

Williams, Dr. Yosef ben-Jochannan, Molefi Asante, Jayne Cortez, Sonia Sanchez, et al, was a cause for grave concern as liberation movements blazed on the African continent.

From various sectors of the Third World and the African Diaspora came the ideas of Frantz Fanon, Cheikh Anta Diop, Ivan Van Sertima, Walter Rodney, Jan Carew, all of which captured some of the earlier conclusions presented by C.L.R. James, George Padmore, and Claudia Jones.

In his book *Black Intellectuals—Race and Responsibility in American Life (*W.W. Norton & Company, 1996)*)* William M. Banks plows through this terrain of thought from the Talented Tenth, to Manning Marable, Adolph Reed, Lani Guinier, Angela Davis, Henry Louis Gates, Gerald Horne, Nell Irvin Painter and several provocative stops along the way.

To some degree UCBerkeley's Dr. Banks' ideas embrace those offered by Professor Watts. His conception of intellectuals “focuses on individuals who are reflective and critical, who act self-consciously to transmit, modify, and create ideas and culture.”

As you can see that’s a pretty wide expanse of concept, and much too often Banks’ focus slants toward academia.

On the other hand, Jacob Carruthers in his *Intellectual Warfare* (Third World Press, 1999) takes on those critical of African-centered thought and ideas. His invocation of the names of George James, Asa Hilliard, James Spady, Dr. Leonard Jeffries, Howard professor Frances Cress Welsing, David Walker, and all the way back to ancient Kemet with the innovations of Imhotep, provides a telling counter to the intellectual tradition fostered by Paul Johnson, whose *Intellectuals (*Harpercollins, 1989*)* attempts a similar recounting, though essentially Eurocentric with James Baldwin and Richard Wright the only black intellectuals in his book.

A cursory glance at my bookshelf reveals some of the scholars and thinkers who have been influential in my intellectual development—Malcolm X, Gordon Parks, Robin Kelly, Charles Ogletree, Peniel Joseph, Ishmael Reed, Derrick Bell, bell hooks, Mumia Abu-Jamal, Fred Beauford, Shirley Graham Du Bois, George Curry, Maulana Karenga, Dr. Ron Daniels, Don Rojas, Malik Chaka, Todd Burroughs, Jared Ball, John Hope Franklin, Maya Angelou, Robert Allen, Baraka, Dan Aldridge, Ron Lockett, Madhubuti, Larry Neal, Glen Ford, Nellie Bailey, Joanna Fernandez, Ossie Davis and Ruby Dee, E. Franklin Frazier, John A. Williams, and John Henrik Clarke—for starters.

Each of us has an extensive list of black intellectuals who have helped us understand the world, and who have shaped the ideas, forged the concepts, and did the deep and critical thinking in the world we inhabit.

Lay out your own trajectory, list your teachers and comrades, and we can compare them the next time we meet. And as Anna Julia Cooper reminded us eons ago, so much depends on when and where you enter this discourse on black intellectuals.

If this brief survey doesn't ignite some feedback, some bracing reaction, then it fails in one of the key precepts of intellectual thought—to deliver an analysis that one can either seize on and embellish, or summon enough gumption to oppose.

There is no way to predict the direction of black intellectuals nowadays. One thing for certain, there will come a time, when perhaps out of total exasperation and anomie, they will turn on each other like crabs in a barrel. When we can overcome the internal contradictions and settle on a plan to bring about an end to institutional racism and the often-infantile quarrels that divides us, we will have a confederacy of comrades on the ramparts for change and prosperity.

Black intellectuals you have nothing to lose but your indifference!

Foxy: My Life in Three Acts

by Pam Grier with Andrea Cagan

Reviewed by Loretta H. Campbell

Most Becoming Legend

What makes a woman a legend? Is it beauty? Is it brains? Should she be multi-lingual? What about sexy? Suppose she's Pam Grier, and she's all these things and more? The answers are in the questions. Grier, queen of, and a survivor from the blaxploitation film era, continues to be one of the most gifted actresses of her generation. Yet her talents have been barely tapped. In *Foxy: My Life in Three Acts, A Memoir*, she outlines the gifts that brought her fame.

It begins with humor about what could have been a fatal accident involving the infant Pam Grier and her entire family.

"...our Buick flipped over three times and came to a stop at the side of the [New Jersey] turnpike, its wheels beneath it. ...That was my first stunt." While she admits the story was recounted to her, her tongue in cheek humor comes across. Her commitment to family is also evident early in the book. Grier was an army kid because her father was a life-long soldier. He moved his family from bases around the country and the world. As a result, Pam picked up various European languages and a love of many peoples and cultures. Her parents were of multi-racial backgrounds and raised their children to be unbiased and accepting of others.

In some ways, this attitude made Grier a target. She describes her love of books and learning. Clearly a bright child, she was also curious and trusting. When asked to come into a room where some of her male cousins were playing, she went. Her cousins raped her. She was six. As she explains later in the book, this was the first time she was raped. There is a disclaimer at the beginning that speaks to this: "I have modified the identities and certain details about some of the individuals described in this book."

This is a chilling statement. Clearly, it was designed to protect the family from the kind of shame brought on by young boys like this. Years later, when she was 18, Grier was raped again. This time it was by a boy called Brian on a prom date. He is described as a kind of "church boy," meaning he had deceived people into believing he was a good kid

Although the trauma of both rapes made her a stutterer, she never lost her love and trust of those who were worthy of both. In her descriptions of everything from the men in her life to her career, Grier comes across as forgiving and spiritual. As she outlines it, her way of coping with trauma was to befriend animals. In particular, she developed a love of horses.

Because Grier's maternal grandparents owned a farm, she often rode the horses there. One horse in particular helped ease her pain after the first assault. He was too big for most of the adults to ride, yet Grier felt a kinship with him. One day, she climbed up on a fence and mounted the horse as he grazed on the family's property. "Big Horse walked over to a massive oak tree and stopped there beside a small pond. I was amazed when I looked into the water and saw my reflection—a tiny girl on top of a huge horse that stood at least eighteen hands." Think of a dinner plate on top of a refrigerator, and you'll get the picture.

Nearly 20 years later, her love of animals stood her in good stead. Fortunately, Grier has worked as a stunt woman with and without animals. In the Italian movie *The Arena* (aka, The Naked Warriors), she accidentally rode another horse of near mythic proportions. For reasons never made clear, a handler caused the horse to gallop almost to his death and to take Grier with him. Because of her work with animals and her martial arts training, she was able to "tuck and roll" when the horse threw her.

Renowned director Federico Fellini was filming a movie nearby and saw her galloping over various movie sets. He was impressed with Grier's riding ability. The two promised to talk about making a film, but the discussion never happened.

Although it was not to be, Grier had nothing to worry about in terms of career opportunities. To begin with, she sings and plays the piano. In the chapter "Going Gospel," Grier talks about her love of gospel music and the racist teachers who refused to teach her to read music, sing, or dance. She learned all three skills despite them.

After her parents' divorced, Grier, her mother, and younger brother struggled with financial and racial obstacles.

The small family settled in Denver. Mrs. Grier, a nurse, was determined that her children get the things they deserved. She attempted to enroll Grier in horseback riding lessons, but the teacher refused to teach her. Luckily, Grier had already learned from her grandparents.

Still, when it came to piano lessons, the problem of finding a teacher seemed insurmountable, until a woman named Mrs. Heinemann stepped in. According to Grier, Mrs. Heinemann overheard one teacher refuse to teach Pam because she was Black. “I’ll give your daughter private lessons,” she told Grier’s mother, “if you can get hold of a piano.” Grier’s grandfather, a semi-pro musician, owned a piano. Thus began her private piano lessons.

She describes Mrs. Heinemann as an accomplished musician and a respected teacher who often arranged for recitals for her students. When she tried to arrange recitals for Grier, they were refused. Grier was talented enough, but white bigots didn't want to hear a Black child play the piano. Happily, Grier's mother was undeterred again. She got her daughter involved with gospel music. This led to singing and playing gospel and later to touring with a gospel choir.

Years later, her singing skills earned her a place as a backup singer for Sly and the Family Stone and as part of Wonderlove, Stevie Wonder's backup group.

Whether singing or working clerical jobs, Grier's work ethic was strong as this book testifies. She proudly explains her willingness to work at whatever job she could to support herself and to attend college.

Her initial career goal was to be a veterinarian. Without money, she had little chance of achieving her dream, or so she thought. Consequently, she often worked two or three jobs at once to save money. Finally, she followed a suggestion to enter a beauty pageant because she would earn enough for college. She won. In some respects that pageant changed the course of her life.

She eventually went to Los Angeles, still in pursuit of college, and landed a job working as a receptionist for a Hollywood agent. One day, another agent stopped by her desk and suggested she audition for Roger Corman, the head of New World Pictures.

"I walked into the audition room shyly and said a quiet "Hello" to Roger, Jack, and a few people who were assisting them. Then I read the words on the page they handed me. ...Roger offered me the role on the spot." This was the early 1970s and the beginning of her movie career. Her two most famous movies from that period, *Coffy* and *Foxy Brown* are considered classics of the genre. Numerous movies, plays, television shows, and stunts were to follow in rapid and regular succession.

As her career was on the upswing, her love life was on the downswing. She describes in detail the rise and fall of her relationships with Kareem Abdul Jabar, Freddie Prinze, and the most horrific, with Richard Pryor. In the chapter, "An Unlikely Couple," she talks about the man behind the celebrity. Pryor was also raped at age six and molested often in the whore house in which he was raised. Because he only went as far as the sixth grade, she tells us, Pryor was nearly illiterate. Yet, he was a comedic genius. Sadly, he was also a drug addict. So strong was his addiction to cocaine that he carried it in his sperm.

In the chapter, "The C Word," Grier shares about her battle with cervical cancer. The chapter implies that Pryor's semen caused this illness. She never blames him. He was a victim who never recovered, and Grier helps us to pity him. Because of her resources, financial and spiritual, Grier was able to embark on a healing program that saved her life. Her strongest support came from her mother and a network of friends. Part of the healing process was her incredible ability to not be bitter.

On the mend, she continued to act, receiving nominations and awards from the NAACP, Golden Globes, and others. Her take on the blaxploitation films that fostered her accolades is moving. “To me, what really stood out in the genre were women of color acting like heroes rather than depicting nannies or maids. We were redefining heroes as school teachers, nurses, mothers, and street smart women who were proud of who they were.”

Now, cancer free, her career moves at a steady clip. She is a mainstay on award winning television shows and regularly works in film and theatre. Hers is a remarkable life. Yet, throughout *Foxy* she is humble and grateful. She thanks the friends who have made her life full. She appreciates her mother’s love. She looks forward to each new adventure. In many ways, the book is a testament to the rewards of being a decent human being. There are good times and bad, but life is to be lived. Grier does so with gusto. That may be why she has achieved the status that she has.

Loretta H. Campbell is a writer, teacher and activist with the New York office of the National Writer's Union.

www.ingramcontent.com/pod-product-compliance
Lightning Source LLC
Chambersburg PA
CBHW021238060726
47590CB00005B/1808
* 9 7 8 1 9 2 9 1 8 8 2 7 7 *